Against Equality

Prisons Will Not Protect You

Against Equality is an online archive, publishing, and arts collective focused on critiquing mainstream gay and lesbian politics. As queer thinkers, writers and artists, we are committed to dislodging the centrality of equality rhetoric and challenging the demand for inclusion in the institution of marriage, the US military, and the prison industrial complex via hate crimes legislation.

This archive can be accessed online at
www.againstequality.org

Against Equality

Prisons Will Not Protect You

Edited by Ryan Conrad

Published by:

Against Equality Publishing Collective, 8 Howe Street, Lewiston ME 04240.

Cover design by:

Chris E. Vargas - www.chrisevargas.com

Dedicated to all the queer and trans folks
engaged in the desperate search for our
most fantastic queer histories...

CONTENTS

Acknowledgements

This project would not have been possible without the endless hours of writing and editing done by all our contributors and those that continue to take a chance on publishing our work. Many thanks to Alternet, The Bilerico Project, *Upping the Anti*, *Workers World Paper*, the National Center for Reason and Justice, PolitiQ-queers solidaires!, the Sylvia Rivera Law Project, AK Press, and the numerous personal blogs on which our work has been posted and re-posted. Additional gratitude goes to Yasmin Nair and Deena Loeffler for their many hours of proofreading and exquisite humor.

Their Laws Will Never Make Us Safer

Dean Spade

An Introduction

At many Transgender Day of Remembrance events, a familiar community anecdote surfaces. The story goes that convicted murderers of trans people have been sentenced to less punishment than is meted out to those convicted of killing a dog. In Istanbul, where trans sex workers have been resisting and surviving severe violence, criminalization, and displacement caused by gentrification, recent advocacy for a trans-inclusive hate crime law has included sharing stories of trans women being raped by attackers who threaten them with death and openly cite the fact that they would only go to prison for three years even if they were convicted of the murder. These stories expose the desperate conditions faced by populations cast as disposable, who struggle against the erasure of their lives and deaths.

The murder of Trayvon Martin in 2012 raised related dialogues across the U.S.. The possibility that Martin's murderer would not be prosecuted, and the awareness that anti-black violence consistently goes uninvestigated and unpunished by racist police and prosecutors, led to a loud call for the prosecution of George Zimmerman. In the weeks after Martin's murder, I heard and read many conversations and commentaries where people who are critical of the racism and violence of the criminal punishment system struggled to figure out whether it made sense to call on that system to make Martin's murderer accountable for his actions.

On the one hand, the failure to prosecute and punish Zimmerman to the full extent of the law would be a slap in the face to Martin's family and everyone else impacted by racial profiling and anti-black violence. It would be a continuation of the long-term collaboration between police and perpetrators of anti-black violence, where the police exist to protect the interests of white people and to protect white life and operate both to directly attack and kill black people and to permit individuals and hate groups to do so.

On the other hand, given the severe anti-black racism of the criminal punishment system, what does it mean to call on that system for justice and accountability? Many people working to dismantle racism identify the criminal punishment system as one of the primary apparatuses of racist violence and probably the most significant threat to black people in the U.S. Opposing that system includes both opposing its literal growth (the hiring of more cops, the building of more jails and prisons, the criminalization of more behaviors, the increasing of sentences) and disrupting the cultural myths about it being a "justice" system and about the police "protecting and serving" everyone. For many activists who are working to dismantle that system, it felt uncomfortable to call for Zimmerman's prosecution, since the idea that any justice can emerge from prosecution and imprisonment has been exposed as a racist lie.

The tensions inside this debate are very significant ones for queer and trans politics right now. Increasingly, queer and trans people are asked to measure our citizenship status on whether hate crime legislation that includes sexual orientation and gender identity exists in the jurisdictions in which we live. We are told by gay and lesbian rights organizations that passing this legislation is the best way to respond to the ongoing violence we face—that we need to make the state and the public care about our victimization and show they care by increasing surveillance of and punishment for homophobic and transphobic attacks.

Hate crime laws are part of the larger promise of criminal punishment systems to keep us safe and resolve our conflicts. This is an appealing promise in a society wracked by gun violence and sexual violence.[1] In a heavily armed, militaristic, misogynist, and racist society, people are justifiably scared of violence, and that fear is cultivated by a constant feed of television shows portraying horrifying violence and brave police and prosecutors who put serial rapists and murderers in prison. The idea that we are in danger rings true, and the message that law enforcement will deliver safety is appealing in the face of fear. The problem is that these promises are false, and are grounded in some key myths and lies about violence and criminal punishment.

Five realities about violence and criminal punishment are helpful for analyzing the limitations of hate crime legislation (or any enhancement of criminalization) for preventing violence or bringing justice and accountability after it has happened:

3

1. **Jails and prisons are not full of dangerous people, they are full of people of color, poor people, and people with disabilities.** More than 60% of people in U.S. prisons are people of color. Every stage and aspect of the criminal punishment and immigration enforcement systems is racist—racism impacts who gets stopped by cops, who gets arrested, what bail gets set, which workplaces and homes are raided by Immigration and Customs Enforcement (ICE), what charges are brought, who will be on the jury, what conditions people face while locked up, and who will be deported. Most people in the U.S. violate laws (like traffic laws and drug laws) all the time, but people of color, homeless people, and people with disabilities are profiled and harassed and are the ones who get locked up and stay locked up or get deported. Ending up in prison or jail or deportation proceedings is not a matter of dangerousness or lawlessness, it's about whether you are part of a group targeted for enforcement.

2. **Most violence does not happen on the street between strangers, like on TV, but between people who know each other, in our homes, schools, and familiar spaces.** Images of out-of-control serial killers and rapists who attack strangers feed the cultural thirst for retribution and the idea that it is acceptable to lock people away for life in unimaginably abusive conditions. In reality, the people who hurt us are usually people we know, and usually are also struggling under desperate conditions and/or victims of violence. Violence, especially sexual violence, is so common that it is not realistic to lock away every person who engages in it. Most violence is never reported to police because people have complex relationships with those who have hurt

4

them, and the whole framing of criminalization where "bad guys" get "put away" does not work for most survivors of violence. If we deal with the complexity of how common violence is, and let go of a system built on a fantasy of monstrous strangers, we might actually begin to focus on how to prevent violence and heal from it. Banishment and exile—the tools offered by the criminal punishment and immigration enforcement systems—only make sense when we maintain the fantasy that there are evil perpetrators committing harm, rather than facing the reality that people we love are harming us and each other and that we need to change fundamental conditions to stop it.

3. **The most dangerous people, the people who violently destroy and end the most lives, are still on the outside—they are the people running banks, governments, and courtrooms and they are the people wearing military and police uniforms.** Fear is an effective method of social control. Prison and war profiteers fuel racist and xenophobic fears by circulating images of "terrorists" and "criminals." [2] In reality, the greatest risks to our survival are worsening poverty and lack of access to health care, adequate housing, and food. This shortens the lives of millions of people in the U.S. every day, along with the violence of police and ICE attacks, imprisonment and warfare that the US government unleashes every day domestically and internationally, and the destruction of our climate, water, and food supplies by relentlessly greedy elites. If we really want to increase well-being and reduce violence, our resources should not be focused on locking up people who possess drugs or get in a fight at school or sleep on a sidewalk—we should be

focusing on dismantling the structures that give a tiny set of elites decision-making power over most resources, land, and people in the world.

4. **Prisons aren't places to put serial rapists and murderers, prisons *are* the serial rapists and murderers**. If we acknowledge that the vast majority of people in prisons and jails are there because of poverty and racism, not because they are "dangerous" or violent, and if we acknowledge that prisons and jail utterly fail to make anyone who spends time in them healthier or less likely to engage in violence, and if we recognize that prisons and jail are spaces of extreme violence,[3] and that kidnapping and caging people, not to mention exposing them to nutritional deprivation, health care deprivation, and physical attack *is* violence, it becomes clear that criminalization and immigration enforcement increase rather than decrease violence overall.

5. **Increasing criminalization does not make us safer, it just feeds the voracious law enforcement systems that devour our communities.** The U.S. criminal punishment and immigration enforcement systems are the largest prison systems that have ever existed on earth. The U.S. imprisons more people than any other society that has ever existed—we have 5% of the world's population and 25% of the world's prisoners. Our immigration prisons quadrupled in size in the decade after 2001. This hasn't made us safer from violence, it *is* violence.

The fundamental message of hate crime legislation is that if we lock more bad people up, we will be safer. Everything about our current law enforcement systems indicates that this is a false promise, and it's a false promise that targets people of color and poor people for caging and death while delivering large profits to white elites. Many might hope that queer and trans people would be unlikely to fall for this trick, since we have deep community histories and contemporary realities of experiencing police violence and violence in prisons and jails, and we know something about not trusting the cops. However, this same ongoing experience of marginalization makes some of us deeply crave recognition from systems and people we see as powerful or important. This desperate craving for recognition, healing and safety can cause us to invest hope in the only methods most of us have ever heard of for responding to violence: caging and exile. Many of us want to escape the stigmas of homophobia and transphobia and be recast as "good" in the public eye. In contemporary politics, being a "crime victim" is much more sympathetic than being a "criminal." By desiring recognition within this system's terms, we are enticed to fight for criminalizing legislation that will in no way reduce our experiences of marginalization and violence.

In recent years, these concerns about hate crime legislation have gotten somewhat louder, though they are still entirely marginalized by the corporate-sponsored white gay and lesbian rights organizations and mainstream media outlets from which many queer and trans people get their information about our issues and our resistance. More and more people in the U.S. are questioning the drastic expansion of criminalization and immigration enforcement, and noticing that building more prisons and jails and deporting more people does not seem to make our lives any safer or better. Many queer and trans people are increasingly critical of criminalization and immigration enforcement, and are unsatisfied by the idea that the answer to the violence we experience is harsher criminal laws or more police.

Three kinds of strategies are being taken up by queer and trans activists who refuse to believe the lies of law enforcement systems, and want to stop transphobic and homophobic violence. First, many people are working to directly support the survival of queer and trans people who are vulnerable to violence. Projects that connect queer and trans people outside of prisons to people currently imprisoned for friendship and support and projects that provide direct advocacy to queer and trans people facing homelessness, immigration enforcement, criminalization and other dire circumstances are under way in many places. Many people are providing direct support to people coming out of prison, or opening their homes to one another, or collaborating to make sex work safer in their communities. This kind of work is vital because we cannot build strong movements if our people are not surviving. Directly helping each other during our moments of crisis is essential—especially when we do it in ways that are politically engaged, that build shared analysis of the systems that produce these dangers. This is not a social service or charity model that provides people with minimal survival needs in a moralizing framework that separates "deserving" from "undeserving" and gives professionals the power to determine who is compliant enough, clean enough, hard-working enough, or quiet enough to get into the housing, job training, or public benefits programs. This is a model of mutual aid that values all of us, especially people facing the most dire manifestations of poverty and state violence, as social movement participants who deserve to survive and to get together with others facing similar conditions to fight back.

The second kind of work is dismantling work. Many people are working to dismantle the systems that put queer and trans people into such dangerous and violent situations. They are trying to stop new jails and immigration prisons from being built, they are trying to decriminalize sex work and drugs, they are trying to stop the expansion of surveillance systems. Identifying what pathways and apparatuses funnel our people into danger and fighting against these systems that are devouring us is vital work.

The third kind of work is building alternatives. Violent systems are sold to us with false promises—we're told the prison systems will keep us safe or that the immigration system will improve our economic well-being, yet we know these systems only offer violence. So we have to build the world we want to live in—build ways of being safer, of having food and shelter, of having health care and of breaking isolation. Lots of activists are working on projects to do this, for example, on alternative ways to deal with violence in our communities and families that don't involve calling the police since the police are the most significant danger to many of us. Many people are engaged in experimental work to do what the criminal and immigration systems utterly fail to do. Those systems have grown massive, built on promises of safety. But they have utterly failed to reduce rape, child sexual abuse, poverty, police violence, racism, ableism, and the other things that are killing us. Their growth has increased all of those things. So, we have to look with fresh eyes at what actually does make us safer. Some people are building projects that try to directly respond when something violent or harmful happens. Others are building projects that try to prevent violence by looking at what things tend to keep us safe—things like having strong friendship circles, safe housing, transportation, not being economically dependent for survival on another person so you can leave them if you want to, and having shared analysis and practices for resisting dangerous systems of meaning and control like racism and the romance myth.

Some people who are identifying prisons and borders as some of the most significant forms of violence that need to be opposed and resisted by queer and trans politics, are calling for an end to all prisons. For me, prison abolition means recognizing prisons and borders as structures that cannot be redeemed, that have no place in the world I want to be part of building. It means deciding that inventing and believing in enemies, creating ways of banishing and exiling and throwing away people, has no role in building that world. This is a very big deal for people raised in a highly militaristic prison society that feeds us a constant diet of fear, that encourages us from early childhood to sort the world into "bad guys" and "good guys." Our indoctrination into this prison culture deprives us of skills for recognizing any complexity, including the complexity of our own lives as people who both experience harm and do harm to others. Working to develop the capacity to even imagine that harm can be prevented and addressed without throwing people away or putting anyone in cages is a big process for us.

In the growing debate about whether hate crime legislation is something that will improve the lives of queer and trans people, and whether it is something we should be fighting for, we can see queer and trans activists working to develop important capacities to discern and analyze together. This form of discernment is familiar to prison abolitionists, and it is also visible in other areas of queer and trans politics. It is an ability to analyze the nature of an institution or system, rather than just to seek to reform it to include or recognize a group it targets or harms. Abolitionists have long critiqued prison reform, observing that prison expansion usually occurs under the guise of prison reform. Important complaints about prison conditions, for example, often lead to prison profiteers and government employees proposing building newer, cleaner, better prisons that inevitably will result in more people getting locked up.[4] Queer activists have engaged this kind of discernment about reforming violent state apparatuses in our work to oppose the fights for same-sex marriage and the ability to serve in the US military. In this work, we have questioned the assumption that inclusion in such institutions is desirable, naming the existence of marriage as a form of racialized-gendered social control and the ongoing imperial and genocidal practices of the U.S. military. This work is complex, because so many queer and trans people, conditioned by shaming and exclusion, believe that getting the U.S. government to say "good" things about us in its laws and policies, no matter what those laws and policies actually exist to do, is progress. This framing asks gay and lesbian people to be the new face of the purported fairness and liberalism of the United States, to get excited about fighting its wars, shaping our lives around its family formation norms, and having its criminal codes expanded in our names. The ability to recognize that an enticing invitation to inclusion is not actually going to address the worst forms of violence affecting us, and is actually going to expand the apparatuses that perpetrate them whether in Abu Ghraib, Pelican Bay, or the juvenile hall in your town, is one that requires collective analysis for queer politics to grasp.

The Against Equality book projects, of which this book is the third and final, offer us a bundle of tools for building that analysis and sharing it in our networks, for trading in the dangerous ideas that the Human Rights Campaign and the other organizations that purport to represent our best interests are not likely to disseminate. This book, in particular, focuses on how criminalization and imprisonment target and harm queer and trans people, and why expanding criminalization by passing hate crime laws will not address the urgent survival issues in our lives. The most well-funded and widely broadcast lesbian and gay rights narratives tell us that the state is our protector, that its institutions are not centers of racist, homophobic, transphobic and ableist violence, but are sites for our liberation. We know that is not true. We are naming names—even if you wrap it in a rainbow flag, a cop is a cop, a wall is a wall, an occupation is an occupation, a marriage license is a tool of regulation. We are building ways of thinking about this together, and ways of enacting these politics in daily work to support one another and transform the material conditions of our lives.

This compilation originally appeared in 2009 on the website of Black & Pink (blackandpink.org), an LGBTQ group that works towards the abolition of the prison industrial complex.

A Compilation of Critiques on Hate Crime Legislation

Compiled by Jason Lydon for Black & Pink

Many liberal, and even self-proclaimed progressive, organizations are fighting for "hate crime" legislation nationally and state-by-state. The Senate just voted in favor of the "Matthew Shepard Bill." Challenges and critiques are made over and over again by queer/trans/ gender non-conforming folks, people of color, low-income/poor folks, and others most impacted by the many tentacles of the prison industrial complex, yet the campaigns continue on. This document is intended to be a bullet point compilation of materials put out by the following organizations (in no particular order): Sylvia Rivera Law Project, Audre Lorde Project, FIERCE, Queers for Economic Justice, Peter Cicchino Youth Project, Denver Chapter of INCITE! Women of Color Against Violence, Denver on Fire, and the article "Sanesha Stewart, Lawrence King, and why hate crime legislation won't help" by Jack Aponte. The intention behind this document is to present a somewhat simplified critique that can inspire a desire for more information.

If a particular crime is deemed a hate crime by the state, the supposed perpetrator is automatically subject to a higher mandatory minimum sentence. For example, a crime that would carry a sentence of five years can be "enhanced" to eight years.

Plain and simple, hate crime legislation increases the power and strength of the prison system by detaining more people for longer periods of time.

Trans people, people of color, and other marginalized groups are disproportionately incarcerated to an overwhelming degree. Trans and gender non-conforming people, particularly trans women of color, are regularly profiled and falsely arrested for doing nothing more than walking down the street.

If we are incarcerating those who commit violence against marginalized individuals/communities, we then place them behind walls where they can continue to target these same people. It is not in the best interest of marginalized communities to depend on a system that already commits such great violence to then protect them.

Hate crime laws do not distinguish between oppressed groups and groups with social and institutional power.

This reality of the state makes it so that white people can accuse people of color of anti-white hate crimes, straight people accuse queers, and so on. Such a reality opens the door for marginalized people to be prosecuted for simply defending themselves against oppressive violence. This type of precedent-setting also legitimizes ideologies of reverse racism that continuously deny the institutionalization of oppression.

Hate crime laws are an easy way for the government to act like it is on our communities' side while continuing to discriminate against us. Liberal politicians and institutions can claim "anti-oppression" legitimacy and win points with communities affected by prejudice, while simultaneously using "sentencing enhancement" to justify building more prisons to lock us up in.

Hate crime legislation is a liberal way of being "tough on crime" while building the power of the police, prosecutors, and prison guards. Rather than address systems of violence like health care disparities, economic exploitation, housing crisis, or police brutality, these politicians use hate crime legislation as their stamp of approval on "social issues."

Hate crime laws focus on punishing the "perpetrator" and have no emphasis on providing support for the survivor or families and friends of those killed during an act of interpersonal hate violence.

We will only strengthen our communities if we take time to care for those who have experienced or been witness to violence. We have to survive systems of violence all the time and are incredibly resilient. We must focus on building our capacity to respond and support survivors and create transformative justice practices that can also heal the perpetrator (though focusing first and foremost on survivors).

Hate crime law sets up the State as protector, intending to deflect our attention from the violence it perpetrates, deploys, and sanctions. The government, its agents, and their institutions perpetuate systemic violence and set themselves up as the only avenue in which justice can be allocated;

they will never be charged with hate crimes.
The state, which polices gender, race, sexuality, and other aspects of identity, is able to dismiss the ways it creates the systems that builds a culture of violence against marginalized communities as it pays prosecutors to go after individuals who commit particular types of interpersonal violence. Hate crime legislation puts marginalized communities in the place of asking the state to play the savior while it continues to perpetuate violence.

Hate crimes don't occur because there aren't enough laws against them, and hate crimes won't stop when those laws are in place. Hate crimes occur because, time and time again, our society demonstrates that certain people are worth less than others, that certain people are wrong, are perverse, are immoral in their very being.
Creating more laws will not help our communities. Organizing for the passage of these kind of laws simply takes the time and energy out of communities that could instead spend the time creating alternative systems and building communities capable of starting transformative justice processes. Hate crime bills are a distraction from the vital work necessary for community safety.

Passing hate crime legislation will not bring back those who have been killed by hateful violence, it will not heal the wounds of the body or spirit, it will not give power to communities who have felt powerless after episodes of violence.
Organizations like the Human Rights Campaign, National Gay and Lesbian Task Force, and others take advantage of our pain and suffering to garner support for these pieces of legislation. Advocates in the campaigns for hate crime legislation tokenize individuals like Sanesha Stewart

16

[murdered trans woman of color from New York City in 2008] and Angie Zapata [murdered trans woman from Colorado in 2008] while still pushing forward the white, class privileged, gay and lesbian agenda. To truly honor those we have lost and to honestly heal ourselves we must resist the inclination to turn to the state for legitimacy or paternalistic protection; let us use the time to build our communities and care for ourselves.

This statement first appeared on the website of the Sylvia Rivera Law Project (srlp.org) in 2009.

SRLP opposes the Matthew Shepard and James Byrd, Jr. Hate Crimes Prevention Act
Sylvia Rivera Law Project

In October 2009, President Obama signed the Matthew Shepard and James Byrd, Jr. Hate Crimes Prevention Act into law. This law makes it a federal hate crime to assault people based on sexual orientation, gender and gender identity by expanding the scope of a 1968 law that applies to people attacked because of their race, religion or national origin. In support of this goal, it expands the authority of the U.S. Department of Justice to prosecute such crimes instead of or in collaboration with local authorities. The law also provides major increases in funding for the U.S. Department of Justice and local law enforcement to use in prosecuting these crimes—including special additional resources to go toward prosecution of youth for hate crimes.

The recent expansion of the federal hates crime legislation has received extensive praise and celebration by mainstream lesbian, gay, bisexual and transgender organizations because it purports to "protect" LGBT people from attacks on the basis of their expressed and/or perceived identities for the first time ever on a federal level. The Sylvia Rivera Law Project does not see this as a victory. As an organization that centers racial and economic justice in our work and that understands mass imprisonment as a primary vector of violence in the lives of our constituents, we believe that hate crime legislation is a counterproductive response to the violence faced by LGBT people.

Already, the U.S. incarcerates more people per capita than any other nation in the world. One out of every thirty-two people in the U.S. lives under criminal punishment system supervision. African-American people are six times more likely to be incarcerated than white people; Latin@ people are twice as likely to be incarcerated as white people. LGBTs and queer people, transgender people, and poor people are also at greatly increased risk for interaction with the criminal justice system. It is clear that this monstrous system of laws and enforcement specifically targets marginalized communities, particularly people of color.

What hate crime laws do is expand and increase the power of the same unjust and corrupt criminal punishment system. Evidence demonstrates that hate crime legislation, like other criminal punishment legislation, is used unequally and improperly against communities that are already marginalized in our society. These laws increase the already staggering incarceration rates of people of color, poor people, queer people and transgender people based on a system that is inherently and deeply corrupt.

The evidence also shows that hate crime laws and other "get tough on crime" measures do not deter or prevent violence. Increased incarceration does not deter others from committing violent acts motivated by hate, does not rehabilitate those who have committed past acts of hate, and does not make anyone safer. As we see trans people profiled by police, disproportionately arrested and detained, caught in systems of poverty and detention, and facing extreme violence in prisons, jails and detention centers, we believe that this system itself is a main perpetrator of violence against our communities.

We are also dismayed by the joining of a law that is supposedly about "preventing" violence with the funding for continued extreme violence and colonialism abroad. This particular bill was attached to a $680 billion measure for the Pentagon's budget, which includes $130 billion for ongoing military operations in Iraq and Afghanistan. Killing people in Iraq and Afghanistan protects no one, inside or outside of U.S. borders.

We continue to work in solidarity with many organizations and individuals to support people in prison, to reduce incarceration, to end the wars on Iraq and Afghanistan, and to create systems of accountability that do not rely on prisons or policing and that meaningfully improve the health and safety of our communities— especially redistribution of wealth, health care, and housing. A few of the many other organizations doing radical and transformative work to increase the health and safety of our communities include:

- The Audre Lorde Project
- FIERCE
- Incite! Women of Color Against Violence
- Queers for Economic Justice
- Right Rides
- TGI Justice Project
- The Transformative Justice Law Project of Illinois

For these reasons, we believe that a law that links our community's experiences of violence and death to a demand for increased criminal punishment, as well as further funding for imperialist war, is a strategic mistake of significant proportions.

This piece first appeared on alternet.org on August 3rd, 2009.

Do Hate Crime Laws Do Any Good?
Liliana Segura

"We have seen a man dragged to death in Texas simply because he was black. A young man murdered in Wyoming simply because he was gay. In the last year alone, we've seen the shootings of African-Americans, Asian Americans, and Jewish children simply because of who they were. This is not the American way. We must draw the line."—President Bill Clinton, final State of the Union Address, January 27, 2000.

It was a year-and-a-half after the horrific torture-murder of James Byrd Jr., the African-American man who was assaulted, chained to a pickup truck and dragged for three miles by three white men in Jasper, Texas, a crime that the New York Times called "one of the grisliest racial killings in recent American history."

A few months later came the similarly brutal killing of Matthew Shepard, a 21-year-old gay man who was savagely beaten and left to die in Laramie, Wyoming.

The perpetrators in both cases were slapped with severe punishments—life sentences for Shepard's killers, and two death sentences and one life sentence for Byrd's. Nonetheless, in the emotional public upheaval that followed, both cases became rallying cries for the passage of state laws to toughen the sentences for hate-motivated crimes.

On the federal level, laws were already on the books defining race-motivated violence as hate crimes, but the same was not true of crimes against the LGBT community. The Matthew Shepard case would set the stage for a 10-year fight to pass federal hate crime legislation to protect LGBT people. Leading the charge were such influential groups as the Human Rights Campaign, the country's largest gay-rights organization.

Despite the fact that when it came to other issues— "Don't Ask, Don't Tell" or marriage equality—the Clinton administration was no friend of gay rights, the White House and congressional Democrats threw their weight behind hate crime legislation. And no wonder: with Clinton presiding over some of the most expansive criminal justice reforms in U.S. history, anyone lobbying for tougher sentencing in the 1990s was in good company. In Congress, supporting hate-crime laws gave Democrats a chance to look tough on crime while also throwing a bone to the LGBT community.

"We hope Congress will heed this call and put aside politics to protect our nation's citizens from the brutal hate crimes that claimed the lives of Matthew Shepard and James Byrd Jr.," Elizabeth Birch, executive director of the Human Rights Campaign, said in November 1999.

Almost 10 years later, on July 16, 2009, the U.S. Senate finally passed the Local Law Enforcement Hate Crimes Prevention Act, otherwise known as the Matthew Shepard Act, as an amendment to the 2010 National Defense Authorization bill, by a strong bipartisan vote of 63-28. The amendment extends federal hate crime laws to include crimes that target a victim based on his or her "actual or perceived" gender, sexual orientation, gender identity or disability.

The Matthew Shepard Act is likely to be signed by President Obama, marking a major victory for HRC and other groups that have fought hard for it over the past 10 years. But even as many see this is a cause for celebration, nearly a decade after Clinton's final state-of-the-union address urged Congress to "draw the line" on hate crimes, the practical value of hate crime legislation remains dubious.

Despite supporters' contention that they will make vulnerable communities safer, there is little proof that the tougher sentencing that comes with hate crime legislation prevents violent crimes against minority groups. Meanwhile, the U.S. prison system continues to swallow up more and more Americans at a record pace. With 1 in 100 Americans behind bars, is a fight for tougher sentencing really a fight worth waging?

Will Tougher Sentences Deter Hate Crimes?

In 2007, the Dallas Morning News ran an editorial titled "The Myth of Deterrence," which took on the canard that maximum penalties would protect people from violent crime.

In theory, the death penalty saves lives by staying the hand of would-be killers. The idea is simple cost-benefit analysis: if a man tempted by homicide knew that he would face death if caught, he would reconsider.

But that's not the real world. The South executes far more convicted murderers than any other region, yet has a homicide rate far above the national average. Texas's murder rate is slightly above average, despite the state's peerless deployment of the death penalty. If capital punishment were an effective deterrent to homicide, shouldn't we expect the opposite result? What's going on here?

"The devil really is in the lack of details," the paper concluded. "At best, evidence for a deterrent effect is inconclusive, and shouldn't officials be able to prove that the taking of one life will undoubtedly save others? They simply have not met that burden of proof, and it's difficult to see how they could."

The arguments for enhanced sentencing in hate crime legislation takes a similar tack, arguing that tougher sentencing will protect LGBT communities by putting "would-be perpetrators on notice," in the words of the HRC.

But will a white supremacist really refrain from harming another person whom he or she believes to be fundamentally inferior over the distant chance it might mean more jail time? Would Byrd's or Shepard's killers have stopped to rethink their violent, hate-fueled crimes?

"Even as national lesbian-and-gay organizations pursue hate crime laws with single-minded fervor, concentrating precious resources and energy on these campaigns, there is no evidence that such laws actually prevent hate crimes," Richard Kim wrote in *The Nation* in 1999. Ten years later, there still doesn't seem to be a lot of data to support this claim.

In 1999, some 21 states and the District of Columbia had hate crime laws on the books. Today, 45 states have enacted hate-crime laws in some form or other. Yet the trend has not been a lowering of hate crimes. In 2006, 7,722 hate-crime incidents were reported to the Federal Bureau of Investigation in 2006—an 8 percent increase from 2005.

The data:

2,640 were anti-black (up from 2,630 in 2005); 967 were anti-Jewish (up from 848 in 2005); 890 were anti-white (up from 828 in 2005); 747 were anti-male homosexual (up from 621 in 2005); 576 were anti-Hispanic (up from 522 in 2005); 156 were anti-Islamic (up from 128 in 2005).

Hate groups also appear to be on the rise. According to the Alabama-based Southern Poverty Law Center, the number of hate groups has increased by 54 percent since 2000.

Speaking before the Senate vote on July 16, Sen. Patrick Leahy, D-Vt., declared, "this legislation will help to address the serious and growing problem of hate crimes." But as one San Francisco Chronicle columnist recently asked, bluntly: "If hate crime laws prevent hate crimes, shouldn't hate crimes be shrinking, not growing?"

Whether hate crimes are on the rise because more crimes are being classified as such is another question. But the data leave the question of deterrence unanswered.

Regardless, the deterrence argument has been embraced by Democratic politicians. Speaking in favor of the Matthew Shepard Act, Rep. Jan Schakowsky, D-Ill., cited the crimes of Benjamin Nathaniel Smith, a white supremacist who killed two people and wounded nine others in a violent "spree" in 1999, apparently targeting Jews and African-Americans. California Democrat Rep. Mike Honda cited the case of Angie Zapata, an 18-year-old transgender woman who was beaten to death in Greeley, Colorado, last year [2008].

But, as with the Clinton administration, the real political value of this recent round of votes was that it gave politicians a chance to appear tough on crime while also appearing to support gay rights. A number of those Democrats who supported the Matthew Shepard Act have been slow to back measures that would actually bestow equal rights on LGBT people. Sens. Max Baucus of Montana, Kent Conrad of North Dakota and Herb Kohl of Wisconsin, to name a few, all oppose same-sex marriage, yet voted in favor of the Shepard Act.

What's more, a number of Democratic senators who voted for the Shepard Act voted in favor of the Defense of Marriage Act in 1996. Even Nebraska Democrat Ben Nelson, who in 2004 was one of two Democrats to vote in favor of amending the Constitution to limit marriage to heterosexual couples—along with then-Georgia Democrat, and certifiable lunatic, Zell Miller—voted for the Matthew Shepard Act.

Given the years of ad campaigns and political lobbying it has taken to get this legislation through Congress, it seems worth considering whether this is the best use of resources by influential LGBT groups, especially given that, as the Shepard case demonstrated, it is already possible to fully prosecute brutal crimes driven by hate or bigotry.

One expert on hate crimes and deterrence, James B. Jacobs, wrote as far back as 1993: "The horrendous crimes that provide the imagery and emotion for the passage of hate-crime legislation are already so heavily punished under American law that any talk of 'sentence enhancement' must be primarily symbolic."

Many LGBT activists agree. As one blogger argued on Feministing recently: "Putting our energy toward promoting harsher sentencing takes it away from the more difficult and more important work of changing our culture so that no one wants to kill another person because of their perceived membership in a marginalized identity group."

Tough on Crime for Progressives?

In a country that leads the world in incarceration—2.3 million people are lodged in the nation's prisons or jails, a 500 percent increase over the past 30 years—the U.S. criminal justice system most brutally affects those very communities that hate-crime laws, historically, have ostensibly sought to protect.

An example: this summer, a new study found that 1 in 11 prisoners are serving life sentences in this country, 6,807 of whom were juveniles at the time of their crimes.

According to the Sentencing Project, its findings "reveal overwhelming racial and ethnic disparities in the allocation of life sentences: 66 percent of all persons sentenced to life are nonwhite, and 77 percent of juveniles serving life sentences are nonwhite."

When it comes to LGBT communities, it is only recently that the "homosexual lifestyle" didn't itself amount to criminal activity in the eyes of the law. (The Supreme Court only overturned laws banning sodomy in 2003.) And the history of police brutality against gays, lesbians and transgender people is hardly history.

Just this month, a gay couple was detained by police in Salt Lake City merely for kissing. A similar incident in El Paso, Texas, led to five gay men being kicked out of a restaurant because the restaurant did not tolerate "the faggot stuff." "Particularly troubling for the El Paso case is that the security officers actually tried to cite laws against sodomy that were thrown out by the U.S. Supreme Court more than five years ago," pointed out one blogger at Change.org.

The criminal justice system has proved to be particularly brutal when it comes to those who are already behind bars, with violence and segregation regularly targeting gays, lesbians and transgender people.

This summer, news broke that prisoners in a Virginia women's prison were being segregated for not looking "feminine" enough, being thrown into a "butch wing" by prison guards. According to the *Washington Blade*, the Bureau of Justice Statistics "has identified sexual orientation to be the single-highest risk factor for becoming the victim of sexual assault in men's facilities."

Although well-established groups like the HRC, the National Gay and Lesbian Task Force, and Parents, Families and Friends of Lesbians and Gays have poured much energy into hate crime legislation, other, smaller LGBT organizations have opposed them on the grounds that toughening the criminal justice system will do little to further tolerance or equality for LGBT people, particularly given the fact that they continue to be targeted by the very same system.

Many more radical LGBT groups reject hate crime legislation on the grounds that the any further expansion of the criminal justice system is at odds with their fight for human rights.

In a letter this spring to supporters of New York's Gender Employment Non-Discrimination Act (GENDA)—which includes a provision that would enhance sentences for existing hate crimes—a coalition of local advocacy groups wrote: "It pains us that we cannot support the current GENDA bill, because we cannot, and will not, support hate crime legislation."

Rather than serving as protection for oppressed people, the hate crime portion of this law may expose our communities to more danger—from prejudiced institutions far more powerful and pervasive than individual bigots. Trans people, people of color and other marginalized groups are disproportionately incarcerated to an overwhelming degree.

Trans and gender non-conforming people, particularly transwomen of color, are regularly profiled and falsely arrested for doing nothing more than walking down the street. Almost 95 percent of the people locked up on Riker's Island are black or Latino/a. Many of us have been arrested ourselves or seen our friends, members, clients, colleagues and lovers arrested, often when they themselves were the victims of a violent attack.

Once arrested, the degree of violence, abuse, humiliation, rape and denial of needed medical care that our communities confront behind bars is truly shocking, and at times fatal.

The Human Rights Campaign argued that passage of the Shepard Act would "put would-be perpetrators on notice that our society does not tolerate bias-motivated, violent crime." But what happens when the perpetrators are those whose duty it is to supposedly enforce the law?

When Tough on Crime Meets Human Rights

Just before the vote on the Shepard Act on July 16, Alabama Republican Senator Jeff Sessions—an opponent of the legislation who could hardly be less tolerant of LGBT rights—pulled a cynical maneuver: he introduced three last-minute additions to the amendment, which was widely decried as a transparent ploy to derail the legislation.

One of them would make the federal death penalty available for prosecutions of hate crimes, an idea that alarmed the legislation's supporters. "This amendment is unnecessary and is a poison pill designed to kill the bill," reported HRC Backstory (the blog of the Human Rights Campaign).

There's no question Sessions has zero interest in bolstering the hate crime bill. But nor does it seem particularly likely that that his maneuver would "kill the

32

bill." After all, as previously discussed, it has been a long time since Democrats had a problem supporting tough-on-crime legislation.

Regardless of its actual strategic value, many of the groups that fought hard for the hate crime bill have sent messages asking Congress to oppose the Sessions amendment.

"The death penalty is irreversible and highly controversial—with significant doubts about its deterrent effect and clear evidence of disproportionate application against poor people," read a letter signed by a long list of advocacy groups, from the Anti-Defamation League to the HRC to the NAACP, which reminded legislators that "no version of the bill has ever included the death penalty."

The National Gay and Lesbian Task Force, for example, called the death penalty a "state-sponsored brutality that perpetuates violence rather than ending it," saying, "It is long past time to send a clear and unequivocal message that hate violence against lesbian, gay, bisexual and transgender people will no longer be tolerated—but it must be done in a way that saves lives, not ends them."

But in a country with largest prison system in the world and the toughest sentences on the books, this discomfiting run-in between supporters of tougher hate crime legislation and the "ultimate punishment" seemed almost inevitable.

Indeed, it is emblematic of a fundamental flaw at the heart of hate crime legislation: human rights groups that lobby for tougher sentencing may believe that, despite all its ugly dimensions, the criminal justice system can be used for more noble ends, to force bigoted elements within society to change and to protect vulnerable communities. But at the end of the day, it amounts to the same classic "tough on crime" canard, just tailored to more liberal sensibilities.

This piece first appeared online at angrybrownbutch.com on February 20, 2008.

Sanesha Stewart, Lawrence King, and Why Hate Crime Legislation Won't Help
Jack Aponte

I've been out of town and subsequently out of touch for a while now, visiting El Paso with my partner to meet her incomprehensibly adorable two-week-old nephew. But in the midst of the happiness that babies and family and vacation bring, two pieces of tragic news have weighed heavily on my mind. Both of them demonstrate how dangerous and hostile a world this is for people who are trans and gender non-conforming.

On February 10, Sanesha Stewart, a young trans woman of color, was brutally murdered in her apartment in the Bronx. This is tragic and deeply saddening in and of itself, and part of a frightening and enduring pattern of violence against trans people. But because of this woman's identities—trans, woman, person of color, low income— the tragedy doesn't end with her death and the grief of those who knew and loved her. Instead, the mainstream media, specifically the *Daily News*, has managed to add to the tragedy with grossly disrespectful and transphobic journalism—if such garbage can even be called journalism. This, too, is part of a pattern, one that I've written about before. And yet, every time I read another disgustingly transphobic article, I'm still shocked and appalled that some media sources will stoop so low. Even in death, even after having been murdered, trans people are given no respect and are treated as less than human.

In an eloquent and resonating post on Feministe.us, Holly posits a world in which Sanesha Stewart's murder would be treated with respect for the victim and a cold eye for the killer, then contrasts that with the lurid reality:

> There was no respect and no cold eye, none at all. I must be imagining some completely different universe where young trans women of color aren't automatically treated like human trash. Where we all live, business as usual is to make a lot of comments about what the murder victim dressed like and looked like, reveal what her name was before she changed it, automatically assume she's getting paid for sex, and to make excuses for the alleged killer.

Only days after Sanesha was murdered, Lawrence King, a 15-year-old, openly gay, gender non-conforming junior high schooler was shot in the head and killed by Brandon McInerney, a fellow classmate, a 14-year-old boy. McInerney has been charged with first-degree murder and a hate crime, for which he could face a sentence of 24 years to life with an additional three years because of the hate crime status.

It's mind-boggling. Mind-boggling that someone so young could be so severely punished for simply being himself; mind-boggling that someone so young could have so much hatred or anger inside of him that he could kill another kid. Or, as Holly suggests in another post, that perhaps McInerney was not acting out of simple hatred:

> I fear the worst—and the worst would not just be that some homophobic asshole killed a child. There's an even worse worst: that a child is dead, and the other child who pulled the trigger did so because he couldn't deal with his own feelings. And now that second child will be tried as an adult, and another life destroyed.

When crimes like the murders of Lawrence King and Sanesha Stewart occur, I often hear queer and trans advocates call for strong hate crime legislation. In a statement from the Human Rights Campaign about King's murder (mind you, I doubt the HRC would ever release any statement about Stewart's murder), Joe Solmonese reiterated this demand:

> While California's residents are fortunate to have state laws that provide some protection against hate crimes and school bullying, this pattern of violence against gay, lesbian, bisexual and transgender students is repeated too often in schools and communities across America each day. This tragedy illustrates the need to pass a federal hate crime law to ensure everyone is protected against violent, bias-motivated crimes, wherever they reside.

I disagree with this response. I cannot see how hate crime legislation can do anything to protect anyone— queer and trans people, people of color, women, and other victims of hate crimes. Hate crime legislation only works after the

37

fact, after someone has been victimized, hurt, or killed. Hate crime legislation cannot undo what has been done. Nor can it undo what has been done to our society and to the individuals within it: the inscription of hatred, of intolerance, of prejudice upon our psyches. Hate crimes don't occur because there aren't enough laws against them, and hate crimes won't stop when those laws are in place. Hate crimes occur because, time and time again, our society demonstrates that certain people are worth less than others; that certain people are wrong, are perverse, are immoral in their very being; that certain people deserve discrimination, derision, and disrespect.

Perhaps advocates of hate crime legislation believe that such laws would send a message to people that homophobia, transphobia, and other forms of prejudice and hatred are wrong. I don't think it will. How could such laws counteract the prejudices that permeate our society? I seriously doubt that hate crime legislation that is only brought up after someone is hurt or killed can make a dent in the ubiquitous flood of messages that we receive from politicians, religious leaders, the media and pop culture stating that queers and trans people are less deserving of respect and rights than straight and non-trans people. In this country, all signs point to queer people being second-class citizens, and trans and gender non-conforming people being maybe third or fourth-class citizens. That is what sets up a situation where someone is targeted because of their sexuality or their gender identity, just as such dehumanization is what has fueled racist and sexist violence for centuries. And that's simply not going to be undone by hate crime legislation. Attacking a few of the symptoms of hatred while leaving others unhindered and the root causes untouched is never going to change much of anything.

Moreover, hate crime legislation is far too tied up with our unjust judicial system and prison industry. How can we rely on systems that continuously target and abuse people of color, queer folks, and trans folks to protect us from targeting and abuse? Can we really trust the police, the courts, and prisons to protect us when much of the time they're violating our rights, tearing apart our families, and ravaging our communities? Is it likely that hate crime legislation will be applied fairly across the board in a system that consistently fails to treat all people equally? I think not. For communities that often find themselves being victimized by the judicial and prison systems, there can be little to gain in bolstering those systems and giving them more power to imprison, possibly unjustly. For my part, I'm invested in prison abolition, so "protections" that serve primarily to send more people to jail for longer periods of time are counter-intuitive.

In fact, because hate crime legislation involves no analysis of power—it's not legislation against homophobic or transphobic or racist acts, but rather against general hatred in any direction—such laws can even be applied against oppressed people. Now, I'm not defending or condoning acts of violence or hatred perpetuated by oppressed people, nor am I saying that one form of violence is better than the other. But the lack of a power analysis built into such legislation reminds me of accusations of "reverse racism" in that they both completely miss the point. Queer folks, trans folks, people of color aren't disproportionately victimized simply because some individuals hate them: that hatred is backed up, reinforced, and executed by an entire system of institutionalized power that allows and in fact encourages such acts of violence. The lack of acknowledgment of these systems of power in hate crime legislation only reinforces my belief that such legislation is relatively useless in doing anything to stop homophobia, transphobia, racism and other forms of oppression, and therefore won't do much to stop the violence that stems from said oppression.

Hate crime legislation won't bring Sanesha Stewart or Lawrence King back, nor will it protect other trans and gender non-conforming folks and people of color from violence fueled by hate. Instead of reacting to hatred with disapproval after the fact, we need to instill a pro-active condemnation of hatred, prejudice and discrimination into our society. Sure, that's a much more difficult job to do, but it can be done, slowly but surely, and it's the only way we're truly going to protect those who need protection most.

This piece originally appeared online at The Bilerico project (bilerico.com) as two separate articles in 2009 and 2011 that have been edited and updated into one.

Why Hate Crime Legislation Is Still Not a Solution
Yasmin Nair

The Matthew Shepard and James Byrd Act (H.R. 1592) expands the 1969 United States federal hate-crime law to include crimes motivated by a victim's actual or perceived gender, sexual orientation, gender identity, or disability. The bill also requires "the FBI to track statistics on hate crimes" against transgender people.

When I first began writing against hate crime legislation (HCL) in the early 2000s, public opinion appeared to be overwhelmingly in favor of it. It was largely determined, in public discourse, that those against HCL were ogres who hated minorities and that those for it were saviors of the same.

Yet, even with the battle lines drawn so carefully, there have been several ruptures in the public's general attitude towards hate crime legislation, the most significant of which was around the trial of Dharun Ravi for the 2010 suicide of Tyler Clementi. Clementi's suicide prompted the gay community to engage in its usual orgy of demonizing and hatred. It set about portraying Dharun Ravi as a cold-blooded killer who committed a "hate crime" against a gay student.

Lost in the quest to declare this a classic case of "bullying" was a more complex and nuanced understanding of how such a thing had come to be, and lost also were the complicated intersections of class and ethnicity that surrounded the case. As reported by the *The New Yorker's* Ian Parker, Ravi faced charges that could have increase his sentencing: "...shortly before Molly Wei [co-defendant] made a deal with prosecutors, Ravi was indicted on charges of invasion of privacy (sex crimes), bias intimidation (hate crimes), witness tampering, and evidence tampering. Bias intimidation is a sentence-booster that attaches itself to an underlying crime—usually, a violent one."

HCL is a panacea embraced by the left, which seeks easy solutions to the complicated problems facing societies broken by the violence of neoliberalism. Several pieces in this anthology have pointed out the problems with HCL and its furthering of the prison industrial complex. HCL can seem to be the only solution when racial and ethnic minorities and the transgender community confront cases of harassment and/or murder. Yet in reducing deaths to the result of "hatred," we tend to forget that vulnerable communities are not vulnerable solely on account of their perceived identity, but because of a host of intersecting factors, including economic vulnerability. In Chicago, Sex Workers Outreach Project has shown that sex workers on the street have to worry more about harassment and violence from cops than from clients, and they are likely to be targeted precisely because they are seen as undeserving of protection. In other words, they are seen as people whose lives simply don't matter. No amount of sentence-enhancement, like the kind advocated for in the trial of Ravi, is going to help with the multiple vulnerabilities faced by so many. All it does is funnel more people into the prison industrial complex.

In the end, Ravi was sentenced to 30 days, on charges of "invasion of privacy, bias intimidation, witness tampering and hindering arrest, stemming from his role in activating the webcam to peek at Clementi's date with a man in the dorm room on Sept. 19, 2010" and of "encouraging others to spy during a second date, on Sept. 21, 2010, and intimidating Clementi for being gay," as reported by ABC news at the time.

Without the spurious attachment of "invasion of privacy" and "bias intimidation," there would have been no conviction at all. Even several gay commentators wrote against the push for sentencing Ravi, pointing out that this would allow everyone to forget about, for instance, what Clementi had already discussed as his parents' discomfort with his sexuality. In other words, what emerged from the Ravi trial was a disruption in the causality model evoked by HCL, and an evoking of the larger contexts and nuances of the harm done to queers.

No one can deny that particular groups are in fact treated with discrimination and even violence. But rather than ask how about how to combat such discrimination and violence, we've taken the easy route out and decided to hand over the solution to a prison industrial complex that already benefits massively from the incarceration of mostly poor people and mostly people of color. It's also worth considering the class dynamics of hate crime legislation, given that the system of law and order is already skewed against those without the resources to combat unfair and overly punitive punishment and incarceration.

Let's be honest: we already think that bigots and "haters" are just "low-class punks and thugs" anyway. It's easy to put a twenty-year-old Latino from Chicago's Pilsen neighborhood in jail for six to ten years because he yelled "fag" while stealing a gay man's wallet. Does that solve the problem of homophobia and bigotry in the boardroom? Do we even have ways to discern and address the latter?

What do we when the violence is committed by the system itself? What do we do with the case of Victoria Arellano, a transgender undocumented immigrant who died shackled to her bed in Immigration and Customs Enforcement detention in 2007 after being denied her AIDS medication? Does the system that brought about her death have a way of accounting for its own "hate crime?"

Hate crime legislation has a murky history already detailed by other writers. But it's worth remembering that one reason it's so popular today is that it's often the only way for some marginalized groups to claim recognition as groups, and to seek redress for the very real violence their members experience in everyday life.

At this point, for instance, the issue of violence against the transgender community is seen as a real threat. Indeed, the only way for trangender people to gain recourse from the criminal legal system is to invoke the language of HCL; in effect, transgender identities are brought into being only through narratives of their erasure. But do we address that violence by helping the state to perpetrate more violence against the most marginal who already fill our jails? Or do we think of better ways to address the consequences of bigotry and prejudice? How do those of us struggling to make sense of what often seems like the overwhelming violence surrounding queer and trans bodies in particular work with the seeming contradictions of wanting that violence to end while faced with the criminal legal system as the only option?

Eric A. Stanley writes, in "Near Life, Queer Death: Overkill and Ontological Capture" in the journal *Social Text*, about the conceptual and material ruptures that occur when queer bodies are mutilated and dismembered far beyond the point of death. Yet, even while noting that such deaths are often not entered into the litany of "hate crimes," Stanley points out that HCL is itself a function of the same liberal democratic principles that claim to provide redress:

> 'Reports' on anti-queer violence, such as the 'Hate Crime Statistics,' reproduce the same kinds of rhetorical loss along with the actual loss of people that cannot be counted. The quantitative limits of what gets to count as anti-queer violence cannot begin to apprehend the numbers of trans and queer bodies that are collected off cold pavement and highway underpasses, nameless flesh whose stories of brutality never find their way into an official account beyond a few scant notes in a police report of a body of a 'man in a dress' discovered.

Herein lies our dilemma: our dead are uncounted and unmourned and the only system that exists to help us comprehend the extent of their numbers is the one that exerts that violence upon us in the first place. But surely there is a way out of all this. As Stanley goes on to write, "What I am after then is not a new set of data or a more complete set of numbers. What I hope to do here is to resituate the ways we conceptualize the very categories of "queer" and "violence" as to remake them both."

That is exactly what we must do as we are met with new reports of violence against trans and queer bodies. As I write, the newspapers report yet another murder of a gender-variant person, this one of a Chicago 19-year-old who went by "Tiffany," and who was also identified as Donta Gooden. Immediate responses already echo the same narratives and language: that Tiffany was killed because of her desire to live an "authentic" life and for "who she was." Already, several organizations are calling for this to be classified as a "hate crime."

But as with so many other such murders, we have no proof that Tiffany was actually killed for exercising a "right" to be an "authentic self." Even if gender presentation had been a reason, Tiffany was made far more vulnerable by a system that refused him or her [at this point, it's unclear whether Tiffany actually preferred female pronouns] resources to the most basic needs, like health care.

This will be the easy route out: claim without ever having to prove that Tiffany was murdered because she was being herself, and you get to ignore the vast complexity of the issues that put him or her in danger in the first place.

To be trans usually means being shut out of housing and employment opportunities, and to be denied medical resources. When we decide, erroneously and on a gut level, that someone was killed for their identity, we are ignoring the greater systemic problems that put trans people in danger in the first place. When we place the burden on an individual's identity, we are in effect personalizing greater systemic and societal problems.

In making the claim that people are killed because they are targeted as transgender, the entire HCL industrial complex, including several trans organizations, is reproducing the erasure of the state's violence towards them.

The violence against queers and trans people is comprised of hateful, vicious, and brutal crimes for which there can be no excuse. But there are already legal remedies in place for such crimes: there are punishments for brutality and for murder.

It makes more sense to come to terms with a difficult fact: that the hatred against queer and gender-non-conforming people which incites such brutality is about a deep-seated hatred of the overturning of codes and performances to which people are strangely and deeply cathected, and it's a hatred that flares up without meaning or the comfort of narrative and deep-seated intention. It's true that kind of hatred sometimes becomes an excuse for violence: "I was so deeply disturbed that I couldn't help but beat/kill him/her."

But HCL only presents a way for us to forget that the senseless violence of which we are constantly made aware is exactly that: senseless and brutal. In the end, HCL grants us nothing more than the cold comfort of extended prison sentences or death—in effect, extending the very violence that we claim to abhor.

Is jailing people for their prejudice really going to curtail bigotry and ignorance? Or will it just end up policing thought and filling the coffers of the prison industrial complex?

This piece was first published Jun 21, 2007 in the Worker's World Paper (workers.org) and was subsequently reprinted by the Bay Area NJ4 Solidarity Committee.

Lesbians Sentenced for Self-Defense: All-White Jury Convicts Black Women

Imani Keith Henry

On June 14, four African-American women—Venice Brown (19), Terrain Dandridge (20), Patreese Johnson (20) and Renata Hill (24)—received sentences ranging from three-and-a-half to 11 years in prison. None of them had previous criminal records. Two of them are parents of small children.

Their crime? Defending themselves from a physical attack by a man who held them down and choked them, ripped hair from their scalps, spat on them, and threatened to sexually assault them—all because they are lesbians.

The mere fact that any victim of a bigoted attack would be arrested, jailed and then convicted for self-defense is an outrage. But the length of prison time given further demonstrates the highly political nature of this case and just how racist, misogynistic, anti-gay, anti-youth and anti-worker the so-called U.S. justice system truly is.

49

The description of the events, reported below, is based on written statements by Fabulous Independent Educated Radicals for Community Empowerment (FIERCE), a community organization that has made a call to action to defend the four women, verbal accounts from court observers, and evidence from a surveillance camera.

The attack

On Aug. 16, 2006, seven young, African-American, lesbian-identified friends were walking in the West Village. The Village is a historic center for lesbian, gay, bi and trans (LGBT) communities, and is seen as a safe haven for working-class LGBT youth, especially youth of color.

As they passed the Independent Film Cinema, 29-year-old Dwayne Buckle, an African-American vendor selling DVDs, sexually propositioned one of the women. They rebuffed his advances and kept walking.

"I'll f— you straight, sweetheart!" Buckle shouted. A video camera from a nearby store shows the women walking away. He followed them, all the while hurling anti-lesbian slurs, grabbing his genitals and making explicitly obscene remarks. The women finally stopped and confronted him. A heated argument ensued. Buckle spat in the face of one of the women and threw his lit cigarette at them, escalating the verbal attack into a physical one.

Buckle is seen on the video grabbing and pulling out large patches of hair from one of the young women. When Buckle ended up on top of one of the women, choking her, Johnson pulled a small steak knife out of her purse. She aimed for his arm to stop him from killing her friend.

50

The video captures two men finally running over to help the women and beating Buckle. At some point he was stabbed in the abdomen. The women were already walking away across the street by the time the police arrived.

Buckle was hospitalized for five days after surgery for a lacerated liver and stomach. When asked at the hospital, he responded at least twice that men had attacked him.

There was no evidence that Johnson's kitchen knife was the weapon that penetrated his abdomen, nor was there any blood visible on it. In fact, there was never any forensics testing done on her knife. On the night they were arrested, the police told the women that there would be a search by the New York Police Department for the two men—which to date has not happened.

After almost a year of trial, four of the seven were convicted in April. Johnson was sentenced to 11 years on June 14.

Even with Buckle's admission and the video footage proving that he instigated this anti-gay attack, the women were relentlessly demonized in the press, had trumped-up felony charges levied against them, and were subsequently given long sentences in order to send a clear resounding message—that self-defense is a crime and no one should dare to fight back.

Political backdrop of the case

Why were these young women used as an example? At stake are the billions of dollars in tourism and real estate development involved in the continued gentrification of the West Village. This particular incident happened near the Washington Square area—home of New York University, one of the most expensive private colleges in the country and one of the biggest employers and landlords in New York City. On June 17th, *The New York Times* reported that Justice Edward J. McLaughlin used his sentencing speech to comment on "how New York welcomes tourists."

The Village is also the home of the Stonewall Rebellion, the three-day street battle against the NYPD that, along with the Compton Cafeteria "Riots" in California, helped launch the modern-day LGBT liberation movement in 1969. The Manhattan LGBT Pride march, one of the biggest demonstrations of LGBT peoples in the world, ends near the Christopher Street Piers in the Village, which have been the historical "hangout" and home for working-class trans and LGBT youth in New York City for decades.

Because of growing gentrification in recent years, young people of color, homeless and transgender communities, LGBT and straight, have faced curfews and brutality by police sanctioned by the West Village community board and politicians. On Oct. 31, 2006, police officers from the NYPD's 6th Precinct indiscriminately beat and arrested several people of color in sweeps on Christopher Street after the Halloween parade.

Since the 1980s there has been a steady increase in anti-LGBT violence in the area, with bashers going there with that purpose in mind.

For trans people and LGBT youth of color, who statistically experience higher amounts of bigoted violence, the impact of the gentrification has been severe. As their once-safe haven is encroached on by real estate developers, the new white and majority heterosexual residents of the West Village then call in the state to brutalize them.

For the last six years, FIERCE has been at the forefront of mobilizing young people "to counter the displacement and criminalization of LGBTSTQ [lesbian, gay, bi, two spirit, trans, and queer] youth of color and homeless youth at the Christopher Street Pier and in Manhattan's West Village." (www.fiercenyc.org) FIERCE has also been the lead organization supporting the Jersey Seven and their families.

The trial and the media

Deemed a so-called "hate crime" against a straight man, every possible racist, anti-woman, anti-LGBT and anti-youth tactic was used by the entire state apparatus and media. Everything from the fact that they lived outside of New York, in the working-class majority Black city of Newark, N.J., to their gender expressions and body structures were twisted and dehumanized in the public eye and to the jury.

According to court observers, McLaughlin stated throughout the trial that he had no sympathy for these women. The jury, although they were all women, were all white. All witnesses for the district attorney were white men, except for one Black male who had several felony charges.

Court observers report that the defense attorneys had to put enormous effort into simply convincing the jury that they were "average women" who had planned to just hang out together that night. Some jurists asked why they were in the Village if they were from New Jersey. The DA brought up whether they could afford to hang out there—raising the issue of who has the right to be there in the first place.

The *Daily News* reporting was relentless in its racist anti-lesbian misogyny, portraying Buckle as a "filmmaker" and "sound engineer" preyed upon by a "lesbian wolf pack" (April 19) and a "gang of angry lesbians." (April 13)

Everyone has been socialized by cultural archetypes of what it means to be a "man" or "masculine" and "woman" or "feminine." Gender identity/expression is the way each individual chooses or not to express gender in their everyday lives, including how they dress, walk, talk, etc. Transgender people and other gender non-conforming people face oppression based on their gender expression/identity.

The only pictures shown in the *Daily News* were of the more masculine-appearing women. On April 13th one of the most despicable headlines in the *Daily News*, "'I'm a man!' lesbian growled during fight," was targeted against Renata Hill, who was taunted by Buckle because of her masculinity.

Ironically, Johnson, who was singled out by the judge as the "ringleader," is the more feminine of the four. According to the June 15th *New York Times*, in his sentencing remarks, "Justice McLaughlin scoffed at the assertion made by...Johnson, that she carried a knife because she was just 4-foot-11 and 95 pounds, worked nights and lived in a dangerous neighborhood." He quoted the nursery rhyme, "Sticks and stones will break my bones, but names will never hurt me."

All of the seven women knew and went to school with Sakia Gunn, a 19-year-old butch lesbian who was stabbed to death in Newark, N.J., in May 2003. Paralleling the present case, Gunn was out with three of her friends when a man made sexual advances to one of the women. When she replied that she was a lesbian and not interested, he attacked them. Gunn fought back and was stabbed to death.

"You can't help but wonder that if Sakia Gunn had a weapon, would she be in jail right now?" Bran Fenner, a founding member and co-executive director of FIERCE, told *Workers World*. "If we don't have the right to self-defense, how are we supposed to survive?"

National call to action

While racist killer cops continue to go without indictment and anti-immigrant paramilitary groups like the Minutemen are on the rise in the U.S., The Jersey Four sit behind bars for simply defending themselves against a bigot who attacked them in the Village.

Capitalism at its very core is a racist, sexist, anti-LGBT system, sanctioning state violence through cops, courts and its so-called laws. The case of the Jersey Four gives more legal precedence for bigoted violence to go unchallenged. The ruling class saw this case as a political one; FIERCE and other groups believe the entire progressive movement should as well.

Fenner said, "We are organizing in the hope that this wakes up all oppressed people and sparks a huge, broad campaign to demand freedom for the Jersey Four."

This text originally appeared in French on a 2009 World AIDS Day broadsheet produced by PolitiQ-queers solidaires (http://politiq.wix.com/politiq) in Montreal, Canada. The text was peer reviewed by Bruno Laprade & Maxime De L'Isle.

First Coffins, Now Prison?
Sébastien Barraud for PolitiQ-queers solidaires!

To mark December 1, 2009, PolitiQ-queers solidaires! is denouncing the criminalization of nondisclosure, exposure to, and sexual transmission of HIV. This repressive approach is ineffective, discriminatory, and stigmatizing. We want to live in a society of solidarity where HIV is prevented rather than punished. We will never defeat HIV/AIDS by hiding it behind bars!

In Quebec and Canada, as in all countries with universal access to antiretroviral (ARV) treatment, HIV has become a chronic disease that can be effectively controlled when it is detected in time. Provided they have equal life conditions, people with HIV can have a life expectancy practically equal to HIV-negative people.

We now know that ARV treatments considerably diminish or even eliminate the level of infectiousness in HIV-positive people.[1] Accordingly, if a large majority of HIV-positive people were treated now, the virus could be eradicated in the medium to long term[2], since if one is no longer infectious, one cannot transmit the virus to

57

partners, despite difficulties in consistently using condoms. The remainder of transmissions would be the result of not knowing one's HIV status. In fact, it appears that people who do not know whether they are HIV-positive show less consistent and realistic preventive behaviors than those who know they are HIV-positive.[3] This is why the key to HIV/AIDS prevention, now more than ever, is detection. The maximum possible number of HIV-positive people must be diagnosed. The growing availability of rapid tests is encouraging, and PolitiQ supports this.[4] However, from our point of view, the lives that HIV-positive people face do not at all encourage these means of protection. The ostracism and violence that people who know they are HIV-positive face—in particular, criminalization—makes these measures ineffective. How can we hope for people to take responsibility by being tested when they will clearly face prejudice and discrimination if they test positive?

This being the case, PolitiQ-queers solidaires! calls for concrete work in coalition to ensure the social and economic conditions needed to ensure that nobody has to be afraid of the consequences a positive result.

1) Providing accurate and up-to-date information on the biomedical and day-today consequences of being HIV-positive. Everyone needs to understand that it is possible to live normally with HIV and that an HIV-positive person is not just a dangerous infectious agent allowed to walk around free. This logically means informing young people as soon as possible, i.e. before they begin their sexual lives. Since in our opinion education is fundamental to a struggle against HIV and against discrimination against HIV-positive people, PolitiQ denounces the abolition of sexual education and sexual health classes in high schools and demands their immediate reinstatement.

2) Fighting still harder against prejudice against HIV-positive people. This prejudice, like all irrational discriminations, stigmatizes and isolates people. This damages self-esteem and eliminates the drive to care for oneself and others. Why be socially responsible when society discriminates against you and rejects you socially and sexually? Living in a society that discriminates against HIV-positive people is a major obstacle towards revealing one's HIV status, an absolute necessity for negotiating safer-sex practices. Even though the overwhelming majority of HIV-positive people are responsible (a 2006 U.S. study found that 95% of HIV-positive people have not transmitted the virus[5]), it is logical that numerous people prefer not to know their HIV status rather than live with the stigma of being HIV-positive.

3) Fighting against the criminalization of exposure to and transmission of HIV. Why would someone be tested if the consequence is to become a potential criminal? This legal pressure is a terrible obstacle to prevention and is therefore grossly counterproductive in the struggle against HIV. It clearly works against our public health and reinforces social HIV discrimination more than ever.[6]

But even beyond the negative impact on the fight against HIV that brings us together today, PolitiQ also wants to raise the other harmful consequences of the criminalization of nondisclosure, exposure to and sexual transmission of HIV.

What about other transmissible diseases? Will transmitting the human papilloma virus (HPV), with which 75% of Canadians are estimated to be infected during their lifetime[7], and responsible for many cervical, uterine, and colorectal cancers, be criminalized? What about hepatitis B and C, or even herpes? Will people be able to sue their co-worker if they don't get vaccinated against a (H1N1) flu?

Does it make any sense, under the Charter of Rights, to legally require a person to consistently reveal their HIV status? Isn't medical privacy a fundamental value of our society and an equality guarantee for all citizens, ill or not? We are concerned about universal access to diagnosis, care, and health care being called into question.

Since certain ethnic and sexual minorities who are particularly affected by HIV/AIDS (Haitians, Africans (especially women), migrants, sex workers, prisoners, trans* women and men who have sex with men) are already afflicted by discrimination due to their identity, does it make sense to add another source of stigmatization to those members of these groups who are HIV-positive? Sex workers are under extreme pressure from their clients not to use condoms, and their work and lives are already criminalized more than enough! This is not meant to dismiss the suffering of people infected with HIV in clearly fraudulent situations (false HIV testing, hiding treatments, etc.). People in these situations have a legitimate right to compensation for the moral and possibly physical harm they have undergone. But why in criminal court? Aren't there other means of redress available, as there were for contaminated blood? Remember that 1,200 Canadians became HIV-positive and 12,000 contracted hepatitis C in the tainted blood scandal—but nobody was ever criminally convicted![8] Why should all HIV-positive people be punished while only a small minority have ever transmitted HIV at all, and only a tiny handful have ever transmitted it truly intentionally? Why place all the responsibility for preventing sexual transmission of HIV on HIV-positive people alone, eliminating shared responsibility—"protect yourself, protect your partner"—which has been the chief preventive principle since the beginning of the pandemic?

Love, ignorance, and law have never protected anyone from any virus or disease. But information, equality, and solidarity have always improved people's well-being and ability to care for themselves and others. With the limits of prevention and the need to diversify to reach all forms of sexuality, penalization will not solve anything: courts cannot do the work of schools!

This piece first appeared online at Friends of Justice (bobchatelle.net) in the summer of 2012.

The Devil in Gay Inc.: How the Gay Establishment Ignored a Sex Panic Fueled by Homophobia

James D'Entremont

While striving to enhance penalties for homophobic thought-crimes, the gay mainstream has been tossing people harmed by some of the worst excesses of homophobia overboard. In the 1980s and '90s, a wave of baroque child-molestation trials steeped in bias against sexual minorities swept the U.S. In response, LGBTQ organizations sometimes joined in virtual lynchings. More often, they maintained a silence interrupted only by the mantra, "We are not child molesters."

Scores of day-care workers, nursery school teachers, baby-sitters and others imprisoned on false sex-abuse charges during the height of the child-protection panic have been exonerated and freed, but a number of almost certainly innocent people convicted of sex crimes against children remain under lock and key. Among them are four women from San Antonio, Texas, now in their second decade of incarceration.

The women's ordeal began in September, 1994, when Serafina Limon caught her granddaughters, Stephanie and Vanessa, in apparently sexualized play with naked Barbie dolls. When Serafina reported this scene to her son Javier, the girls' father, he concluded the girls, aged seven and nine, had been exposed to lesbian sex at the home of their aunt. Police were informed. The girls were brought to the Alamo Children's Advocacy Center for evaluation. Following an investigation, Javier's estranged partner's younger sister, Elizabeth Ramirez, 19, and three of her friends were charged with multiple counts of aggravated sexual assault.

In July, Liz Ramirez's nieces had spent a week at her San Antonio apartment. During that period, a Latina lesbian couple, Anna Vasquez and Cassandra "Cassie" Rivera, had visited, bringing with them Cassie's children. Liz's roommate, Kristie Mayhugh, was also present. Neighbors' children ran in and out of the apartment. Days passed without incident. When the girls returned home, they showed no signs of trauma.

The chief investigator was a homicide detective, Thomas Matjeka, who had never previously interviewed children thought to have been sexually abused. He made no recordings of his sessions with Stephanie and Vanessa, who had already been grilled by others including their father. Interrogating Liz Ramirez, Matjeka told her that although she currently had a boyfriend, he knew about her sexual history of involvement with women, implying that homosexuality made her a menace to children.

The case took a long time to go to trial. Elizabeth Ramirez was tried separately and convicted in February, 1997. Having previously been offered ten years' probation in exchange for a guilty plea, she received a prison term of 37 years and six months. A year later, Anna, Cassie, and Kristie were tried together, found guilty, and given

64

15-year sentences. At both trials, prosecutors repeatedly alluded to the defendants' sexual orientation, implying it was a short step from lesbianism to child rape. There was minimal evidence except the uncorroborated testimony of Liz Ramirez's nieces, who recited carefully prepped claims that the women had pinned them down and inserted objects and substances including a tampon and a strange white powder into their vaginas.

The women, who have come to be known as the "San Antonio Four" or the "Texas Four," have gained a growing number of supporters convinced they are innocent. Few of those advocates belong to the gay community of San Antonio, a city that ironically, according to the 2010 U.S. census, has the highest concentration in the U.S. of lesbian parents raising children under 18.

In scores of trumped-up cases dating back to the early '80s, police claimed to have apprehended groups of caregivers conspiring to have sex with children entrusted to their care. The abuse scenarios, often confabulated through coercive questioning of child witnesses, were given a diabolical spin. Investigative journalist Debbie Nathan, co-author of *Satan's Silence: Ritual Abuse and the Making of a Modern American Witch Hunt,* has called the San Antonio Four debacle "probably the last gasp of the Satanic ritual abuse panic."

Somewhere in the long, rich pageant of American brutality, there may indeed have been instances of devil-worshippers sexually abusing children. But the Satanic ritual abuse (SRA) pandemic was made of thin air. Rigorous investigations, some by law enforcement officials eager to unearth a vast Satanic underground, have shown that no such network exists. As historian Philip Jenkins states in *Moral Panic: Changing Concepts of the Child Molester in Modern America,* "The SRA movement represents an eerily postmodern dominance of created illusion over supposedly objective reality—what Baudrillard would term the stage of pure simulation."

The nonexistence of SRA in the real world didn't prevent it from becoming a staple of junk journalism and daytime talk shows. The implausibilities of self-proclaimed SRA survivors' narratives didn't lessen the fervor with which belief in SRA was promoted by such "experts" as New York psychiatrist Judianne Densen-Gerber, founder of the Odyssey House drug-rehabilitation chain, and such public personalities as Geraldo Rivera, Oprah Winfrey, and Gloria Steinem. "Believe It!" trumpeted *Ms.* magazine. "Cult Ritual Abuse Exists!"

The phenomenon owed a great deal to the 1980 publication of *Michelle Remembers,* in which Michelle Smith, a patient of Canadian psychiatrist Lawrence Pazder, described how she had, through treatment, overcome traumatic amnesia to access awareness of childhood abuse by the ubiquitous, powerful "Church of Satan." Michelle remembered being raped, locked in a cage, forced to witness human sacrifice, and smeared with fresh blood.

The book was a bestseller. Eventually exposed as fraudulent, *Michelle Remembers* followed such '70s pulp-psych blockbusters as the multiple personality/recovered memory saga *Sybil* into popular consciousness. The pseudo-memoir validated rumors that thousands of cultists were subjecting thousands of children to outré sexual assault. Both the Smith/Pazder book and *Sybil* helped popularize the idea that although countless people had, as children, been subjected to ritualistic kinky sex, most required therapeutic intervention to recall such horrors. That notion gave rise to a huge, lucrative, now compellingly debunked therapy movement centered on repressed memory.

SRA allegations were excluded from evidence presented to both juries at the trials of the San Antonio Four, but belief in that phenomenon shaped pre-trial investigations. Examining pediatrician Nancy Kellogg, respected co-founder of the Alamo Children's Advocacy Center, was a true believer in SRA. In her medical reports on Stephanie and Vanessa, Kellogg stated that she had notified the police that the abuse, which she was convinced took place, might well have been "Satanic-related."

The principal mass sex-abuse scares of the SRA era involved "sex rings" and imagined predation at child-care facilities. Many of the alleged abusers were said to be manufacturing child pornography, although no child porn linked to SRA cases was ever found and used as evidence. Most of the sex-abuse trials flouted standards requiring presumption of innocence and determination of guilt beyond a reasonable doubt.

In *Sex Panic and the Punitive State* (2011), Roger N. Lancaster asks, "[D]o overblown fears of pedophile predators represent new ways of conjuring up and institutionally using homophobia, even while disavowing it as motive?" Typically, late 20th-century witch hunts began with allegations tinged with homophobia even when the principals were straight. A man, perceived as gay, with children directly in his care—or working in close proximity to children—would be suspected of having preyed upon at least one boy. There was a widespread assumption that any man who sought work with very young children *must* be gay.

The panic was launched in 1982 when a volley of accusations echoed through Kern County, California, where fabricated evidence pointed to half a dozen active sex rings in and around the city of Bakersfield. Thirty-six people were arrested and convicted of child rape. One of the harshest sentences, 40 years, went to gas plant foreman John Stoll, convicted of 17 counts of molesting five boys.

In 1983, as the Bakersfield sex-abuse frenzy wore on, the hysteria spread southeast to the L.A. suburb of Manhattan Beach, site of the McMartin Pre-School. The McMartin case, which morphed into the longest, costliest criminal process in U.S. history—a marathon ending in no convictions—started with a schizophrenic's fantasy that Ray Buckey, the founder's grandson, had sodomized her two-and-a-half-year-old son. Seven McMartin employees were implicated in a host of imaginary crimes including kiddie-porn photo shoots and dark, perverted rites in nonexistent tunnels. Michelle Smith and Lawrence Pazder appeared on the scene to advise prosecutors and comfort parents.

Lurid publicity sparked fresh accusations. In late September 1983, about three weeks after the McMartin case began to snowball, authorities in Jordan, Minnesota, began delving into allegations that 24 adults and one teenager held orgies involving over 30 children, including infants. By 1984, the contagion had reached Massachusetts. Gerald Amirault, whose mother ran the Fells Acres Day Care Center near Boston, was accused of raping a four-year-old boy; he and his mother and sister were imprisoned for a host of crimes against children, including production of never-located child pornography. As the Amirault investigation came to a boil, a 19-year-old gay child care worker, Bernard Baran, was arrested in Pittsfield at the opposite end of the state.

The child-molestation panic that spread across the U.S. in the 1980s had gay-specific antecedents. These included two high-profile witch hunts targeting largely imaginary cabals of gay men. One tore through Boise, Idaho, in 1955; the other hit the Boston area in 1977-78.

In Boston, anti-gay dread was incited and amplified by Christian citrus-industry shill Anita Bryant's "Save Our Children" campaign, a Florida-based propaganda blitz against gay rights ordinances. Bryant's chief message was that gay men and lesbians target children for conversion to the "homosexual lifestyle." As John Mitzel notes in *The Boston Sex Scandal* (1980), the Save-Our-Children panic was given respectable secular underpinnings by Dr. Judianne Densen-Gerber of Odyssey House, who proclaimed that child pornography was rampant and mainly the work of rapacious queers. In California, meanwhile, State Senator John Briggs railed against gay teachers, accusing them of "seducing young boys in toilets."

At the heart of the Massachusetts furor was a man in Revere, a Boston suburb, who had been letting friends and acquaintances use his apartment as a discreet place to bring male hustlers for sex. Suffolk County's paleo-Catholic District Attorney, Garrett Byrne, 80, learned of the arrangement and ordered a crackdown. Local rent boys were rounded up and ordered to name their johns. Thirteen cooperated. Little more than the depositions of two fifteen-year-old hustlers were finally used to indict two dozen men for over 100 sexual felonies. The lives of the accused adults were shattered, although only one—Dr. Donald Allen—went to trial. Allen received five years' probation; only the man who supplied the apartment did prison time. Most of the streetwise young men corralled by Garrett Byrne were above the state's legal age of consent, 16, though at a time when sodomy laws could be enforced at the whim of the enforcer, age of consent was almost beside the point.

The scandal owed much of its heat to the input of Boston-based pediatric nurse Ann Burgess, who created a diagnostic sex-ring model widely applied in the '80s and

'90s, from the Bakersfield circus to the 1994-'95 panic in Wenatchee, Washington, where 43 adults, including parents and Sunday school teachers, were held on 29,726 false charges of sexual abuse. Burgess asserted that international gay sex rings were flying boys to secret locations where they could be ravished. Although most of the child-protection books she wrote or edited, such as *Child Pornography and Sex Rings* (1984) and *Children Traumatized in Sex Rings* (1988), have dated badly, Burgess now teaches victimology and forensics at Jesuit-run Boston College. She remains influential. One of her pupils, Susan Kelley, played a key role in the Amirault case, interviewing children by means of leading questions and "anatomically correct" dolls, refusing to take *no* for an answer.

In 1978, Boston activists formed the Boston/Boise Committee, out of which grew two organizations that survive. One was the North American Man-Boy Love Association (NAMBLA), originally focused on relationships between adult men and adolescents, now demonized out of all proportion to the varied predilections of its minuscule membership. The other was Gay and Lesbian Advocates and Defenders (GLAD, not to be confused with the anti-defamation group GLAAD). Created as a legal resource for gay people accused of sex crimes, GLAD long ago ceased to deal with criminal cases, choosing instead to work usefully on HIV/AIDS and gender identity issues, and less usefully on marriage rights and hate-crime legislation.

No gay organization of any kind acknowledged the existence of Bernard Baran. The first day-care worker to be convicted of mass molestation, Baran went to trial before the McMartin staff and the Amirault family. He was an openly gay teacher's aide at the Early Childhood Development Center (ECDC) in Pittsfield,

Massachusetts. His original accuser was a woman who had just removed her four-year-old son from ECDC, complaining about the facility's willingness to let a homosexual work with children. The woman and her boyfriend had a history of violence and substance abuse. The investigation, however, yielded tidier accusers. The case took on a measure of *gravitas* when a middle-class mother who taught ceramics at Pittsfield's posh Miss Hall's School for Girls claimed Baran had attacked her three-year-old daughter.

A grand jury was shown edited videotapes of child interviews, omitting extensive footage showing the children being coached, prodded, and offered rewards while they denied everything. Baran's attorney, hired out of the phone book on a $500 retainer, did not object. By the time Baran's trial began in January, 1985, he had been indicted on five counts of rape and five counts of indecent assault and battery against two boys and three girls aged three to five. A third boy was added at trial. The courtroom was closed for children's testimony which, when not incoherent, echoed prompting from prosecutor Daniel Ford. Ironically, the "index child"—Paul Heath, 4, the boy whose mother made the first accusation—was dropped from the case after when he refused to cooperate in court, denying abuse and responding to questions with "Fuck you!"

The prosecution exploited jurors' fears of homosexuality. At a time when the specter of AIDS was everywhere, the Berkshire County D.A. adopted a diseased-pariah strategy. Because Paul Heath had tested positive for gonorrhea—according to a test now known to produce a high rate of false positives—Ford brought in a physician to testify to the prevalence of gonorrhea among prostitutes and homosexuals. It didn't matter that Baran's gonorrhea tests came back negative. Paul Heath had, in fact, recently made a more credible disclosure of abuse by one of his mother's boyfriends, a likelier source of STD. Word that this allegation was being investigated never reached Baran's lawyer.

In his closing argument, Ford described Baran's "primitive urge to satisfy his sexual appetite." Given access to children, he continued, Baran acted "like a chocoholic in a candy factory." Found guilty on all counts, Baran received three concurrent life sentences. Sent to the maximum-security state prison at Cedar Junction, he was savagely raped on arrival. He had repeatedly been offered—and refused—five years of low-security incarceration in exchange for a guilty plea.

Similar cases with homophobic overtones kept finding their way into court. Prosecution of lesbians for ritualistic sex abuse was rare, but hardly unknown before the arrest of the San Antonio Four. Women enmeshed in sex-ring hysteria were often accused of assaulting young girls. At the 1988 trial of Margaret Kelly Michaels, prosecutors devoted two days to exploiting a same-sex relationship in her personal history, implying that lesbianism had impelled her to force toddlers of both sexes to lick peanut butter off her cervix at the Wee Care Nursery School in Maplewood, New Jersey.

Some abuse trials may have been impacted by anti-gay propaganda swirling around seemingly unrelated issues. In February 1998, at the time of the second San Antonio Four trial, a local funding controversy was still raging.

In 1997, San Antonio talk-radio host Adam McManus and a Christian horde campaigned to end city funding of the Esperanza Center for Peace and Justice. The effort was triggered by disapproval of Esperanza's *Out at the Movies* film festival, a queer film series the center had been running annually for six years. Correspondence received by the City Council stressed that Esperanza "intends to use some of the money… to indoctrinate our impressionable youth to [the gay] lifestyle." Esperanza's city funding was cut from $62,531 to zero.

"I love homosexuals," declared right-wing activist Jack Finger, railing against Esperanza at a September, 1997, City Council meeting. "What I absolutely hate is the evil, wicked, child-seducing lifestyle."

San Antonio's gay community did not rally around Esperanza during the uproar. The left-leaning, Latina-headed resource was not a lesbigay organization *per se;* it represented a range of minorities. Also, relations between its director, Graciela Sanchez, and the wealthy, white gay business establishment had become strained.

Esperanza, in turn, seems to have taken little notice of the San Antonio Four. That situation finally changed in December 2010, when *La Voz de Esperanza,* the center's newsletter, ran an article by Tonya Perkins defending the four women and noting the "homophobia which poisoned San Antonio in the 1990s." At this writing, Esperanza remains the only officially gay-connected entity in Texas or beyond to call attention to the injustice. There has been no self-designated gay publication in San Antonio since 1997; the gay press elsewhere in Texas—including *Dallas Voice*, Houston's *OutSmart*, and *This Week in Texas* (*Twit*)—has been mostly silent on the San Antonio Four.

Austin-based documentarian Deborah Esquenazi, who is making a film about the San Antonio Four, says local and national LGBTQ organizations have generally ignored her efforts to contact them. "Mostly," she says, "they don't respond to emails and phone calls."

Esquenazi's experience with Gay Inc. echoes that of others—including this writer working on behalf of

Bernard Baran—who have tried to enlist the aid of such groups as the Human Rights Campaign in raising awareness of wrongfully convicted queers—or the treatment of queer prisoners, innocent or guilty. Lambda Legal, the primary LGBTQ legal resource nationally, chooses to focus on "impact litigation," not criminal justice.

"Gay people intersect with the criminal justice system in all kinds of ways," says New York activist Bill Dobbs, co-founder of the anti-assimilationist, pro-sex organization Sex Panic. "But when one of us gets accused of a crime, the leadership goes mute. The focus on victims has blinded us to serious injustices."

The San Antonio Four's predicament was mainly brought to light by people and organizations that are not gay-identified. Canadian researcher Darrell Otto discovered the case while sifting through reports on female child molesters, and became certain the women were innocent. He traveled to Texas, established a website (www.fourliveslost.com), wrote articles and blog entries on the subject, and secured the sponsorship of the National Center for Reason and Justice (NCRJ), an organization devoted to reversing wrongful convictions. *Satan's Silence* co-author Debbie Nathan, then a board member of the NCRJ, helped convince the Texas Innocence Project to take the case. Articles began appearing in the *Texas Monthly* and elsewhere.

"At first, I thought, well, maybe those women did it," says Deborah Esquenazi, "but once we'd sifted through the whole case, we were sure they're innocent. My partner and I realized that could be us."

Esquenazi and others who examined the case found the investigation flawed, the evidence meager, and the court proceedings tainted by prejudice. During jury selection,

Elizabeth Ramirez's lawyer allowed at least two individuals with moral antipathy to homosexuality to be seated as jurors—including the man elected foreman. At her sister-in-law Anna's trial, where prosecutor Mary Delavan linked lesbianism to abuse of little girls, Rose Vasquez counted at least 75 sometimes pointedly derogatory references to lesbians. As the trial progressed, Rose and her husband signed a notarized affidavit stating they overheard a juror discussing "lesbians assaulting two children" at a restaurant with a county employee. Although the affidavit should have caused the juror's removal, the document dropped into a void.

None of the San Antonio Four was subjected to the psychological testing and evaluation processes administered to accused sex offenders in most jurisdictions. Nowhere was it noted that Javier Limon had accused others of molesting his daughters, or that—despite his vocal distaste for lesbians—Javier had been writing love letters to Liz Ramirez, who had rejected him. His letters, which still exist, were never entered into evidence. There were also unacknowledged inconsistencies in the girls' unevenly rehearsed testimony. At Elizabeth Ramirez's trial, Vanessa swore her aunt had held a gun to her head while she talked with her father on the phone and told him all was well. During the trial of the other three women, Vanessa said Anna Vasquez held the gun.

As Darrell Otto notes in his blog, "[M]ost juries find child witnesses to be highly credible, in spite of the fact that it has now been shown that children often lie on the witness stand, for a variety of reasons."

At sex abuse trials, children have been accorded privileges that sometimes trump the rights of the accused, including special seating arrangements concealing them from their alleged abusers, closed courtrooms, and testimony by

CCTV or by proxy. At many of these trials, spoon-fed statements by child witnesses have comprised the prosecution's entire case. Yet there is widespread recognition among social scientists and legal professionals that the familiar exhortation to "believe the children" can render egregious results. In *Jeopardy in the Courtroom*, their 1995 book on child testimony, psychologists Stephen Ceci and Maggie Bruck were among the first to show how aggressive and suggestive questioning of non-abused children can lead to "non-victimized children making false disclosures."

A recent breakthrough for the San Antonio Four was the recantation of Stephanie, Elizabeth Ramirez's younger niece, who now says she was told she would "end up in prison or even get my ass beaten" if she didn't recite a claim of abuse she knew to be untrue. There is now hope that even in Texas, a state where poor and working-class defendants are at a notorious disadvantage, the San Antonio Four will be exonerated as well as freed. It helps that they now have the competent legal representation they lacked at trial.

For the moment, however, the women remain in the maw of the largest—and perhaps most rigidly authoritarian—state penal system in the U.S. According to the March 23, 2012, issue of *Dallas Voice,* Texas leads the nation in prison rape, and "LGBT prisoners are 15 times more likely to be raped." Amid the regimentation and the threat of violence, the women remain resistant to declarations of guilt and shows of remorse that could facilitate parole. Branded "in denial," sex offenders who fail to cooperate with treatment may be vulnerable to one-day-to-life civil commitment.

"[One] condition of parole is to complete a sex offender program…," wrote Anna Vasquez in 2007. "I will not take the coward's way out to just go home."

It takes special bravery for queers to negotiate the American criminal justice system, where homophobia seems encoded in the institutional DNA. In a study published in 2004 by *The American Journal of Criminal Justice*, 484 Midwestern university students were polled on attitudes toward lesbians and gay men. Despite most students' inclination to extend some rights to gay people, criminal justice majors were found to have a higher degree of anti-gay prejudice than students majoring in any other field. Homophobia among criminal justice professionals, like racism, vitiates the official charge to serve and protect everyone, without exception.

In U.S. prisons, systemic homophobia often has an evangelical dimension. Born-again Watergate felon Charles Colson's anti-gay Prison Fellowship Ministries has been preaching to literally captive audiences nationwide since 1975. The Kansas correctional system, which matches state prisoners with "faith-based mentors," employs many hard-line fundamentalist Christians, including members of Topeka's Fred Phelps clan, whose website is www.godhatesfags.com. Margie Phelps, Director of Re-entry Planning for the Kansas Department of Correction, is an anti-gay firebrand whose favorite homophobic epithet is "feces eater."

"When I went to prison," says Bernard Baran, who survived rapes and beatings in several facilities, "I suddenly didn't have a name. I was 'Mo,' short for 'Homo.' In the joint, gay people are at the bottom of the heap. If they think you're a gay child molester, you're the lowest of the low."

Baran finally gained his freedom after unedited videos of child interviews—hidden from both the jury and his lawyer during his trial—were finally unearthed in 2004 a few months after the sudden death of Berkshire County D.A. Gerard Downing, who had claimed for years the tapes were missing. In 2006, his conviction was overturned on grounds of ineffective assistance of counsel. Baran was freed. In 2009, he won a resounding Appeals Court victory, after which all charges were dropped.

Baran spent 21 years and five months in prison. Many of those caught in the child-abuse panic fared better. As the Jordan, Minnesota, case unraveled, all defendants but one were freed. All but two of the Bakersfield defendants were released on appeal. John Stoll, among the last, was released in 2004 when four of his supposed victims, who had been pressured into telling investigators what they wanted to hear, finally recanted. The Amiraults were freed under onerous conditions enabling prosecutors to save face, but at least permitted to return home. Margaret Kelly Michaels's conviction was overturned five years into a 47-year sentence. Others, including the allegedly child-murdering West Memphis Three, have walked out of prison in a state of near or total vindication.

Others remain behind bars. Among them are some of the priests caught in the wide net of the Roman Catholic sex-abuse scandal. These include gay ex-priest Paul Shanley, 81, convicted in 2004 on the unsubstantiated "recovered memories" of a steroid addict. (Street lore falsely credits Shanley with founding and participating in NAMBLA; he did, on the other hand, found the Boston chapter of Dignity, which has disowned him.) A number of dubious, unresolved sex-abuse cases persist in Texas. Besides the San Antonio Four, there is the 1992 SRA case of Austin day-care proprietors Fran and Dan Keller, now serving 48-year sentences.

Those still in prison have, however, acquired a growing number of queer advocates. Additional rays of hope have appeared the form of queer-specific prisoner outreach efforts like Black and Pink, and events like the watershed

2010 Chicago symposium "What's Queer About Sex Offenders? Or, Are Sex Offenders the New Queers?" Increasingly, queer activists recognize the ways in which the prison industrial complex degrades us all. There is a growing awareness that in the U.S., many people are serving time for crimes they did not commit, and that everyone trapped in the world's most populous and retentive chain of gulags is subject to cruel and unusual punishment.

But there is a long way to go. In working exclusively on behalf of putative victims, the LGBTQ mainstream has been strengthening and refining the powers of a system that has traditionally nurtured and sheltered homophobic bias, a system that has long been the surest, sharpest means of keeping sexual minorities in line.

This piece first appeared in issue 13 of the Canadian journal Upping the Anti (uppingtheanti.org) in 2011.

"Worst of the Worst"? Queer Investments in Challenging Sex Offender Registries

Erica R. Meiners, Liam Michaud, Josh Pavan, Bridget Simpson

Points of Departure

Over the past thirty years, Canada and the United States have afforded select gays and lesbians more rights, both symbolic and substantial. Simultaneously, most mainstream gay and lesbian organization have disengaged from the issues of prisons and policing. Resisting police brutality, pushing back against the criminalization of non-heteronormative sexualities, and fighting carceral expansion have each disappeared from queer rights organization's ostensible agendas. Given that most queers are no longer viewed as the "worst of the worst sexual offenders," mainstream gay and lesbian organizations have disengaged from questions of criminalization in order to "move on" to other issues like marriage and military inclusion. Meanwhile, sex workers, the HIV positive, barebackers, and other sexually marginalized groups have become increasingly isolated. With carceral expansion becoming an important priority for Canada's governments, and with "sex offenders" increasingly being used to legitimate "tough on crime" policies and prison growth, intersectional interventions on prison issues that include a queer analysis are needed now more than ever.

Federal and provincial governments in Canada are currently set to expend massive amounts of capital to enlarge the carceral apparatus by constructing new prisons and expanding existing ones. This development is accompanied by increased policing, new surveillance technologies, post-release reporting and registration requirements, and other punitive tools that activists and academics have described as a "soft extension" of the prison industrial complex into everyday life. "Sex offenders" and public notification systems have played a pivotal role in bolstering demands for increased surveillance of public places, extensive post-release requirements, and—at times—community notification. The anxieties propagated by "sex offenders" increase the policing of sexually marginalized people, increase the number of charges and convictions, and lengthen prison terms. These fears also spur electoral campaign promises, moral panics that collude with racialized and heteronormative agendas, and persistent punitive requirements that require various levels of government to appear "tough on crime." In turn, these responses lead to demands for new prisons. As notification technologies shift from print to online databases, offender information has begun to circulate increasingly rapidly and widely. Activists attempting to counter misinformation are often shut out from these platforms and potential roles for a critical independent media are circumvented. The potential for broader based community mobilizations is thus limited.

Although there has been some opposition to tough–on–crime social policy in Canada over the past few years, the organized left has been largely silent on this particular front; even activists traditionally critical of crime-and-punishment approaches have allowed themselves to be seduced by the state's ideas about the "sex offender."

Linking the targeting of homosexuals in the past to contemporary sex offender registries should not be mistaken for a romantic appeal to celebrate outlaw sexualities. Nor do queer peoples' histories of being labeled "sex offenders" guarantee an automatic political affinity with those who are currently being criminalized.[1] However, these histories are intertwined with contemporary carceral growth. While select queers are no longer explicitly targeted by public policies, new "sexual offender" legislation does increase queer vulnerability and queer exposure to imprisonment. Meanwhile, the most significant forms of sexual violence (intimate and familial violence) become obscured by the state's focus on "stranger danger" and "dangerous sexual offenders." Equally obscured are the endemic rates of sexual (and other forms of) violence that incarcerated people— overwhelmingly poor, indigenous, and people of colour— are subjected to within prisons. Most importantly, the state's response to "sex offenders" does not address persistent interpersonal sexual violence, which is perpetrated largely by men, and which largely harms women and children.

As justice organizers, educators, advocates, abolitionists, and (in some cases) as survivors of violence, we engage in an analysis of the state's response to sexual and gendered violence with care. We view this moment of carceral expansion as an opportunity to map overlaps between queer and abolitionist politics and to support community-based responses to state and interpersonal sexual violence.

Sex Offender Registries and Carceral Expansion

Over 2.3 million people are now incarcerated in prisons and jails across the United States. This works out to one in every 99.1 adults. Compared to all other nations, the U.S. has the highest rate of imprisonment and the largest number of people locked behind bars. Disproportionately, they are people of color and poor people. Since the 1970s, incarceration rates have increased—not because of rising levels of violence or crime but because of (among other things) "three strikes" laws, mandatory minimum sentencing, and the war on drugs.

Canadian prison expansion has followed a similar trajectory. In 1986—just days after a similar announcement by Ronald Reagan—Prime Minister Brian Mulroney announced Canada's own war on drugs. Prison populations exploded, necessitating the construction of new penal institutions across the country. Decades of overcrowding in the provincial and territorial systems also led to the construction of new prisons and additions to existing facilities. The criminalization of the survival economy accounts for an ever-growing proportion of the offenses for which individuals are incarcerated: in 2008-2009, over 90% of incarcerated women were serving time for prostitution, small theft (valued under $5,000), or fraud. Under the federal Conservatives, the Correctional Service of Canada's (CSC) annual budget has increased by 1.385 billion (86.7%), almost doubling since 2005-2006. As of June 2011, various provincial and territorial correctional authorities have announced plans for additions to existing facilities and the construction of twenty-two new prisons.[2]

Prison expansion in the U.S. and Canada is increasingly marketed as a response to the "worst of the worst"—

those who commit acts of violence (generally sexual) against the "most innocent," white children. Over the last two decades, sex offender registries (SORs) and community notification laws have been one of the most visible fronts in the expansion of the U.S. carceral state. Public fears about "sex offenders" (SOs) during the 1990s coincided with the construction of supermax, or control-unit, prisons.[3] Although there is no evidence that these registries and notification systems reduce persistent sexual violence against children and women, the policing of public spaces like parks and school grounds have increased along with people's anxieties.

Throughout the 1990s, the U.S. federal government passed laws requiring states to develop SO registries, to increase community notification systems, and to integrate and standardize processes for tracking and identifying those convicted of sexual offenses. In 1996, in response to the abduction and murder of twelve-year-old Polly Klaas (1992) and seven-year-old Megan Kanka (1994) by two men with prior convictions for violent sexual crimes, the federal government passed Megan's Law. The law established a publicly accessible national sex offender registry that circulated information about known "sex offenders" across the nation. It also coordinated the then-emergent state registry systems.

SORs restrict employment, housing, and mobility—particularly in public and private spaces where children congregate. These laws have been tested in and supported by the courts, and more punitive measures continue to be introduced; upheld by the U.S. Supreme Court in a 2005 decision, civil commitment laws have given law enforcement the power to incarcerate those convicted—even after the completion of their formal sentence. Encouraged by media coverage of child abductions, restrictions on convicted sex offenders increase despite the fact that most perpetrators of sexual and other forms of violence against children are family members.

Over the past ten years, there has been a steady push for a more aggressive national sex offender registry in Canada. Initially introduced as a provincial initiative in 2001[4] by the Harris Conservatives in Ontario, Christopher's Law was the political response to the rape and murder of an 11 year-old boy by a man on statutory release. Under pressure from the provinces, the federal government followed suit in 2004 by establishing the National Sex Offender Registry. In 2007, a 62,000-signature petition was presented to the National Assembly in Québec demanding a province-wide and publicly accessible database. Tied to broader "tough on crime" policy shifts, the Conservatives introduced Bill S-2 (Protecting Victims from Sex Offenders Act) in the spring of 2010. The bill includes provisions that would make registration mandatory, give police preventative access, and require those recently-registered to provide DNA samples. The stated purpose of Bill S-2 is to "strengthen the National Sex Offender Registry and the National DNA Data Bank by enabling police in Canada to more effectively prevent and investigate crimes of a sexual nature." A federal attempt to coordinate emerging provincial registries, The National Sex Offender Registry has yet to solve a single crime.[5]

Despite a thirty-year low in Canadian crime rates[6] and little to no evidence of any rise in violence in Canada, the federal Conservatives introduced a schedule of reforms in 2010 that mirrors failed U.S. criminal justice policies: mandatory minimum sentencing, further criminalization of drug offenses, the elimination of pretrial "two-for-one" credits, and new prison construction. Child "protection" against alleged sexual predators is a central component of current criminal justice reforms in Canada.

Bill S-2 and Bill C-22 (Protecting Children from Online Sexual Exploitation Act, which passed first reading in May 2010) are offered to allegedly protect select children. Meanwhile, proposed changes to the Youth Criminal Justice Act will punish more young people. As always, the state's "protection" measures constitute after-the-fact responses and afford no prevention measures. We are thus compelled to question the intent and design of this kind of social policy.

As in the U.S., public fears of the "sex offender" have been leveraged to build the Canadian carceral state. After the Bloc Québécois voted *en masse* against Bill C-268 (which would impose a mandatory minimum sentence for those convicted of child trafficking) in 2009, the federal Conservatives mailed flyers to every resident in each Bloc Québécois riding. Under the headline "Your Bloc MP voted against the protection of children" (in French), the flyer depicted a dark, shadowy man leading a white child from a playground. Concurrently, other print advertisements suggested the Bloc was "soft on pedophiles." In the spring of 2011, the Ontario Progressive Conservatives promised that—if elected—they would make sex offenders wear GPS trackers and make the entire Ontario registry publicly accessible online. Alberta has already implemented a similar GPS tracking pilot project. These moves demonstrate the extent to which public opinion is amenable to highly punitive surveillance and policing where "sex offenders" are concerned. Campaigns for increased criminalization and prison expansion continue to succeed by framing the opposition as "soft" on crime, insensitive to the safety of children, and indifferent to the realities of sexual violence.

In the U.S., opposition to publicly accessible SORs (limited though it is) has been sparked by instances of vigilante violence against accused or convicted sex offenders, targeted harassment and outings, cases of mistaken identity, and limited but detailed investigative journalism that has chronicled the explicitly punitive restrictions on SO movement post-release. In Canada, notable opposition from either the institutional or grassroots left has yet to materialize. This is in large part due to the non-public nature of the Canadian registry, which has allowed it to enact much of the everyday surveillance and restriction of the American registry while avoiding public debates and opposition. By monopolizing mobilizations of disgust and pity, the Canadian state has effectively regulated and managed opposition to how sex offenses are criminalized and administrated.

Queer Investments

The push for the public registration of "sex offenders" evokes familiar queer histories. Many of the frameworks and strategies currently being used to detain, surveil, and punish "sex offenders" are well known by queer activists who have spent decades battling the policing and surveillance of street sex workers, bars and clubs, and bathhouses and other public sexual cultures. Policing in Canada has historically targeted queer people and continues to target sexually marginal and marginalized groups. When select white and affluent gays and lesbians ceased to be the overt targets of policing and queer organizations moved on to other issues, anti-prison communities lost a formidable ally. As public memory of queer resistances to criminalization evaporated, our communities lost their critical assessment of what constitutes "dangerous sexual behavior." How are these designations made? And who is all this "protection" for?

Gay, lesbian, bisexual, and especially transgender, transsexual, and gender nonconforming communities continue to be overrepresented in the Canadian and U.S. criminal justice system, though this vulnerability is no longer (or rarely) the result of explicitly homophobic state violence. Today, prison justice and abolition activists—and queer organizers—struggle with both the implications of relentless prison growth and our diminished capacity to name, identify, and resist the social processes that underwrite this expansion. Because gay and lesbian community organizations have widely disengaged from criminalization, queers are less equipped to contend with shifting patterns of state violence and new articulations of "sex offenses."

Queer Histories

Historically, queers have been the targets of criminal persecution and registration. In many jurisdictions, non-reproductive homosexual sexual acts were *by definition* sex offenses and used to restrict access to employment, social benefits, parenting, immigration, and citizenship. Queer historian William Eskridge has reported how, in 1947, the California legislature "unanimously passed a law to require convicted sex offenders to register with the police in their home jurisdictions." Chief Justice Warren requested that this law be extended to include those convicted of "lewd vagrancy" to ensure that as many homosexuals as possible were included. In 1950, the Federal Bureau of Investigation collected information—including fingerprints—for those charged with sodomy, oral copulation, and lewd vagrancy to create a "national bank of sex offenders and known homosexuals." [7]

However, homosexuals and other "sex offenders" were not uniformly targeted. As Eskridge reports, "in the

1930s, when only 6% of its adult male population was non-white, twenty percent of New York Cities sex offenders were black," revealing who was—and continues to be—most vulnerable to policing and sexual surveillance.[8] In a 1965 case that received national attention in Canada, a Northwest Territories man named Everett George Klippert was charged and convicted on several counts of gross indecency for having consensual sex with several men. In his sentencing, he was deemed to be "an incurable homosexual" and therefore a "dangerous sexual offender" to be placed in indefinite preventative detention.[9]

These historical practices have become central to SORs and are also apparent in contemporary policing of marginal or marginalized sexual cultures. This is especially evident when considering how public notification and shaming—often under the guise of public (and, particularly, childhood) "safety"—are used to target and police sexually marginal social spaces and public sexual cultures. Throughout the early 1980s, hundreds of men in Canada and the U.S. were publicly outed after being caught having sex in public bathrooms, bathhouses, and other sites. Following the Toronto bathhouse raids of 1981, the names of men present during the raid were published in *The Toronto Sun* while police contacted their employers. After targeting a group of underage sex workers and their clients in 1994, police in London, Ontario held press conferences to expose a "sex ring" that "passed around boys." In response, the Homophile Association of London Ontario accused the police of unfairly accusing men, engaging in double standards for gay sex, and promoting exaggerations, distortions, and fear-mongering.[10] Bar and bathhouse raids during the early 2000s (of which there were many) played out similarly.

Public notification and shaming are often legitimated by claims that they protect youth from sexual violence. Nevertheless, for youth engaging in sex work and often for queer youth, protection is negated by the very mechanisms that purport to "protect" youth from sexual exploitation. In 2003, forty Montréal police officers raided Taboo, a gay club featuring stripping and frequented by sex workers and those interested in purchasing non-heterosexual sex. Police arrested and laid indecency charges against four customers and 23 young male strippers (including one seventeen year old). Raids of bars frequented by sex workers or that provide space for public sexual cultures are not exceptional in Canada; however the raid at Taboo is significant because it constitutes what Maria-Belén Ordóñez, a Toronto-based anthropologist, has called a "homophobic response that is mainly tied to young sex workers catering to older gay men."[11] The raids, their rationale, and the court proceedings that followed demonstrate how legal enforcement mobilized to protect youth in fact criminalized young people.[12]

Flexibility of the "Sex Offender" Category

Under Canadian law, the formal "sex offender" designation has gradually been dropped from many sexual practices associated with queers; however, other non-normative sexual practices continue to designated in this way. Sexually deviant archetypes that represent "predatory" or "irresponsible" sexuality—often non-hetero-patriarchal and always deeply racialized—continue to be targeted for state regulation. These include the "welfare queen," the teenaged mom, the HIV+ person who "willfully infects" others, and the sex worker. While "homosexuals" may no longer be the central targets of social policies enforcing sexual normativity, the effects of this policing continue to be felt by many, including queers.

In the U.S., the criminal "sex offender" category is applied inconsistently. In 2010, sex workers in New Orleans were charged under a state-wide law that makes it a crime against nature to engage in "unnatural copulation" (committing acts of oral or anal sex). Conviction meant registration as an SO and having the words "sex offender" stamped on one's driver's license. Meanwhile, out of concern for the futures of the young people, the 3rd U.S. District Court of Appeals in Philadelphia ruled that "sexting" (distribution of pornography) did not warrant felony charges, which would require registration as a sex offender if convicted.[13]

The increasing criminalization of HIV non-disclosure in Canada[14] also demonstrates the uneven and violent application of the "sex offender" classifications. From 1998 to 2011, a slate of charges—ranging from sexual assault to first-degree murder—were brought against HIV+ individuals for having failed to disclose their HIV status. These charges were overwhelmingly laid against immigrants, men of colour, sex workers, and (increasingly) gay men. Their names and photographs have routinely been published in newspapers, even prior to conviction. In 2008, Vancouver police blanketed the downtown core with posters featuring the picture of a sex worker who was merely suspected of having transmitted HIV. In Winnipeg in August 2010, police published a Canada-wide arrest warrant for a Sudanese man *suspected* of transmitting HIV to two women. And in Ottawa in May 2010, police issued a public warning about a gay man accused of non-disclosure during consensual sex and explicitly labeled him a "sexual predator." Many of the charges brought against HIV+ individuals for not disclosing their status during a sexual encounter—sexual assault, aggravated sexual assault, etc.—are grounds for registration on the Canadian SOR. While it remains to be seen to what extent individuals criminalized for non-disclosure will actually be added to the registry (as many of the cases are in progress), recently proposed reforms threaten to add almost all of those facing conviction under HIV-related prosecutions.

The trajectory of HIV criminalization—and, in particular, the tactics of public notification and shaming—reveals how recent legal shifts are firmly rooted in broader historical constructions of the "sexual predator." HIV criminalization exacerbates what geographer Ruth Wilson Gilmore has called "group-differentiated vulnerabilities" to criminalization and imprisonment and premature death.[15] In this way, it mirrors prior public panics about sex offenders and homosexuals, which were characterized by public naming, scapegoating, and widespread social vilification.[16]

Designation and registration of sex workers as "sex offenders," criminalization of sexual non-disclosure of HIV status, and appeals to highly punitive surveillance technologies to contain, monitor, and track known "sex offenders" all resemble the ways in which queer sexuality has been policed and managed historically. While gay and lesbian communities may no longer be targeted explicitly, these communities continue to be subject to state violence and "sex offender" panic as sex workers, as HIV-positive people, and as those to whom the "sex offender" designation has been applied.

Erasure

Registries function to obscure the real sources and sites of sexual violence. Overwhelmingly, the perpetrators of sexual violence against women and children are not strangers. The focus on "stranger danger" functions to displace attention from the real harms: poverty, colonialism, and heteropatriarchy. As anthropologist Roger Lancaster summarizes, "a child's risk of being killed by a sexually predatory stranger is comparable to his or her chance of getting struck by lightening (1 in 1,000,000 versus 1 in 1,200,000)."[17] Despite this reality, U.S. legal scholar Rose Corrigan points out that feminist organizers were largely silent during the implementation of national registries in the U.S. and Canada. In her estimation, "the most threatening aspects of feminist rape law reform—its criticisms of violence, sexuality, family, and repressive institutions—are those that supporters of Megan's Law erase in rhetoric and practice."[18] The "worst of the worst," if there is such a thing, is to be found in our own patriarchal families and neighbourhoods.

In addition to the reality that perpetrators of violence targeting children are rarely strangers, there is no evidence that registries and community notification systems protect children. In Canada, where SORs are non-public and used overwhelmingly to investigate crimes that have already been committed, they cannot—by their own logic— prevent any crime. Criminologists who study these registries have argued that there is no evidence that they have been successful and that their expansion has been "based on a mere verisimilitude of empirical justification."[19] Creating safer and strong communities requires that we challenge the expansion of these registries. By challenging mythic and manufactured sources of sexual violence, we are forced to confront sexual violence in its most widespread, everyday, and intimate forms.

The Carceral State

An increase in criminalization means that those most vulnerable—including queers and those involved in survival economies like the sex and drug trade, people living with HIV, and those that challenge age of consent laws—will be caught up in the criminal justice system. More people in the system means more people subjected to racist, gendered, and homophobic judicial proceedings. Conviction means detention and confinement in institutions predicated on gender normativity, compulsory heteronormativity, and colonial and racial oppression. More people will become isolated from communities of affinity and origin and more will be exposed to epidemic rates of HIV and Hepatitis C in prisons that withhold the resources necessary for survival. Expansion of the carceral state also means increased exposure to state and structural violence through interlocking punitive systems like child protection services, immigration enforcement, psychiatric intervention, and related medical violence.

This deepened exposure to state violence also increases vulnerability to sexual violence. According to one U.S. study, 20 percent of inmates in men's prisons are sexually abused at least once while serving their sentence.[20] Among women at some U.S. prisons, the rate is as high as 25 percent. Violence also occurs in ineffective sexual offender "treatment" programs.[21] Not only does the state's claim to offer protection fall terribly short, it actively produces an array of new possibilities for gender and sexual violence.

Mythic Children

SORs are part of the carceral state's push toward a culture of child protection almost wholly focused on sexual innocence. Across the U.S., as select brown and black boys are moved into juvenile detention centers at age eleven, as queer youth are denied meaningful sexual health education, and as pregnant teenagers are pushed out of school, it's clear that "protection" is unevenly accessed. The laws across the U.S. that protect young children from sexual violence—Megan's Law, Jessica's Law, The Adam Walsh Act, the Amber Alert—almost uniformly refer to white children. Almost by definition, constructions of mythic sexual innocence make queers into threats (even in contexts where individual lesbians and gays may be protected). Poll after poll demonstrates that the public perceives pedophilia to be the greatest threat to childhood safety. This perception is intimately linked to fear of the queer. As queer theorist Lee Edelman put it, "the sacralization of the child thus necessitates the sacrifice of the queer."[22] In a heteronormative culture that valorizes sexual innocence, non-normative sexualities are suspect, contagious, and thought to pose risks.

Queer Futures/Abolition Futures

SORs and the moral and political anxieties they foster are central pathways enabling carceral expansion. The Harper government's recent "tough on crime" legislative changes focused on sex offenses provide yet another example of carceral expansion being enabled by "sex offender" anxieties. Coalitions between queers and prison abolitionists are needed now more than ever as lesbian and gay mainstream organizations restrict their focus to marriage and the military (in the U.S.) and sentencing enhancements for those convicted of hate crimes against gays and lesbians (in Canada). The state's focus on "sex offenders" opens a new front in the regulation of sexual deviance. Proceeding under a banner that effectively inspires loathing and fear, they obscure the historical links between current objectives and homophobic social policy and state violence. Elaborating these links is particularly urgent in the face of current efforts to expand the Canadian carceral state. Most centrally, prison expansion that includes U.S.-style SORs does nothing to make our communities stronger or to reduce or eliminate sexual violence.

Resistance to carceral expansion and SORs must come from a variety of institutional, community, and organizational forces. Organizing against prison expansion requires that we identify how queers are still being harmed by "sex offender" panics and analyze how sexually-related offenses are still being mobilized in the service of the carceral state. Organizing must also support the self-determination of survivors of violence and build accountability for perpetrators without encouraging carceral expansion. Below, we highlight three themes around which to organize these struggles. We believe they offer clear sites for organizing a broader and more effective movement against sexual and state violence. There is other work happening; this list is neither representative nor comprehensive but comprises an assemblage of different models. We learn from a number of organizations doing pieces of this work, and we argue that linking these pieces together can provide a framework for transforming bankrupt notions of state "protection."

1. Direct support for youth (and others) doing sex work. This work is currently being done by groups like Projet d'Intervention auprès des Mineurs-res Prostués-ées

(PIAMP)[23] in Montréal and the Young Women's Empowerment Project in Chicago. These organizations support sexual and other forms of self-determination and autonomy, interrupt multiple violences faced by youth criminalized or otherwise marginalized, and challenge the ideas of "predatory sexuality" and childhood innocence that fuel prison expansion. Recognition of youth as potential sexual actors and broader support for sexual self-determination for youth disrupts the state's mobilization of childhood innocence to legitimize further violence and sexual regulation in the name of "protection."

2. *Engagement with sexual violence without turning to the state*. This work is currently being done by groups like Generation Five and the Storytelling and Organizing Project in Oakland and the Challenging Male Supremacy Project in New York. These organizations are working to build community-based reconciliation and develop mechanisms and practices of accountability for those that perpetrate harm. Specifically, they strive to build collective responses to harm that are rooted in queer, anti-racist feminism and that don't create or reproduce vulnerability to state and sexual violence. By examining the sites and sources of sexual violence, these projects offer tools for survivors, elaborate frameworks that connect interpersonal violence to state violence, and develop responses outside of the frameworks of state punishment. These responses are intended to be transformative for survivors, "bystanders," and those that perpetrate harm.

3. *Case support, individual advocacy, and direct support for individuals convicted under SO provisions*. This work is currently being one by groups like the National Center for Reason and Justice in Boston and the Prisoner Correspondence Project in Montréal. The advocacy of

these organizations challenges the myth that criminalization actually functions to "catch" the "worst of the worst." Work of this nature exposes how the punitive structures of the carceral state do little to address persistent sexual and gender-based violence. It also shows how socially sanctioned practices of vilification and scapegoating often increase sexual and gender violence through overexposure to imprisonment.

These organizations offer us models for imagining and building a cross-community coalitional politics to confront claims that imprisonment is an effective response to sexual violence. They build processes that contend with sexual and intimate violence while rejecting how the state "sees" and responds to violence and conceives of sexual "crimes." Together, they offer us various points of departure from which to imagine and build abolition futures.

Organizations cited in piece

Challenging Male Supremacy Project:
leftturn.org/experiments-transformative-justice

Critical Resistance: criticalresistance.org

Generation Five: generationfive.org

National Center for Reason and Justice: ncrj.org

Prisoner Correspondence Project:
prisonercorrespondenceproject.com

Projet d'Intervention auprès des Mineurs-res Prostués-ées:
piamp.net/

Storytelling and Organizing Project: stopviolenceeveryday.org

Notes

Their Laws Will Never Make Us Safer

[1] A 2011 study published in the *Journal of Trauma-Injury Infection & Critical Care* reported that "[t]he U.S. homicide rates were 6.9 times higher than rates in the other high-income countries, driven by firearm homicide rates that were 19.5 times higher. For 15-year olds to 24-year olds, firearm homicide rates in the United States were 42.7 times higher than in the other countries."

Richardson, Erin G. S.M.; Hemenway, David PhD, "Homicide, Suicide, and Unintentional Firearm Fatality: Comparing the United States With Other High-Income Countries," 2003, *Journal of Trauma-Injury Infection & Critical Care*, January 2011 - Volume 70 - Issue 1 - pp 238-243.

http://journals.lww.com/jtrauma/Abstract/2011/01000/Homicide,Suicide,_and_Unintentional_Firearm.35.aspx.

Every year, approximately 100,000 people in the US are victims of gun violence, and about 85 people per day die from gun violence in the U.S. "Gun Violence Statistics," Law Center to Prevent Gun Violence, http://smartgunlaws.org/category/gun-studies-statistics/gun-violence-statistics/. An average of 207,754 people age 12 or older experience sexual assault every year in the U.S. Approximately every two minutes, someone is sexually assaulted. 54% of assaults are not reported to the police, and 97% of rapists do not serve any jail time. "Statistics," Rape, Abuse & Incest National Network, http://www.rainn.org/statistics/. According to the Colorado Coalition Against Sexual Assault, in the U.S. one out of every six women and one out of thirty three men have experienced an attempted or completed rape. Citing National Violence Against Women Survey, "Prevalence, Incidence, and Consequences of Violence Against Women," November 1998. The Colorado

Coalition Against Sexual Assault also reports that "the United States has the world's highest rape rate of the countries that publish such statistics—4 times higher than Germany, 13 times higher than England, and 20 times higher than Japan" citing NWS, "Rape in America: A Report to the Nation," 1992). See, http://web.archive.org/web/20100822123802/http://www.ccasa.org/statistics.cfm.

[2] It is helpful to remember that people in the U.S. are eight times more likely to be killed by a police officer than a terrorist. "Fear of Terror Makes People Stupid," Washington's Blog, http://www.washingtonsblog.com/2011/06/fear-of-terror-makes-people-stupid.html citing National Safety Council, "The Odds of Dying From…" http://web.archive.org/web/20080508135851/http://nsc.org/research/odds.aspx.

[3] By conservative estimates, 21% of people in men's prisons are estimated to experience forced sex while imprisoned. Cindy Struckman-Johnson & David Struckman-Johnson (2000). "Sexual Coercion Rates in Seven Midwestern Prisons for Men" (PDF). *The Prison Journal* 80 (4): 379–390.

[4] Angela Davis lays out this argument succinctly and effectively in *Are Prisons Obsolete?* Angela Y. Davis, *Are Prisons Obsolete?* (New York: Seven Stories Press, 2003). In 2012, these dynamics were visible when anti-prison activists in Seattle started a campaign to stop the building of a new youth jail that the local government was promoting as a way of resolving long-term complaints about horrible conditions of confinement in the existing youth jail. The anti-prison activists argued that the old jail should be closed, but not replaced. The campaign is ongoing. See, http://nonewyouthjail.wordpress.com.

First Coffins, Now Prison?

[1] Vernazza P, Hirschel B, Bernasconi E, Flepp M. (2008). Les personnes séropositives ne souffrant d'aucune autre MST et suivant un traitement antirétroviral efficace ne transmettent pas le VIH par voie sexuelle. Commission fédérale pour les problèmes liés au sida (CFS), Commission d'experts clinique et thérapie VIH et sida de l'Office fédéral de la santé publique (OFSP): http://www.saez.ch/pdf_f/2008/2008-05/2008-05-089. pdf. In 2012, treatment as prevention (TasP) is now one of the tools with condoms (combinated prevention) to fight against HIV transmission within sero-discordant couples, especially those who want to have babies naturally.

[2] Lima VD, Johnston K, Hogg RS, Levy AR, Harrigan PR, Anema A, Montaner JS. (2008). "Expanded access to highly active antiretroviral therapy: a potentially powerful strategy to curb the growth of the HIV epidemic." *Journal of Infectious Diseases*, July 1st, 198(1), p.59-67.

[3] Burman W, Grund B, Neuhaus J, Douglas J, Friedland G, Telzak E, Colebunders E, Paton N, Fisher M, Rietmeijer C. (2008). "Episodic Antiretroviral Therapy Increases HIV Transmission Risk Compared With Continuous Therapy: Results of a Randomized Controlled Trial," *Journal of Acquired Immune Deficiency Syndrome*, 49, p.142–150.

[4] In 2012, even home testing is in development, since the FDA has just approved Oraquick test: http://www.fda.gov/NewsEvents/Newsroom/PressAnn ouncements/ucm310542.htm.

[5] Holtgrave DR, Irene Hall H, Rhodes PH, Wolitski RJ. (2008). Updated Annual HIV Transmission Rates in the United States, 1977–2006. *Journal of Acquired Immune*

Deficiency Syndrome and Center for Disease Control and Prevention.

[6] In 2012, we know from two studies that HIV criminalization may discourage testing.

O'Byrne P, Bryan A, Woodyatt C, Nondisclosure prosecution and HIV prevention: results from an Ottawa-based gay men's sex survey: https://dl.dropbox.com/u/1576514/O%27Byrne,%20nondisclosure%20prosecutions,%20JANAC,%202012.pdf.

The Sero Project: National criminalization survey preliminary results, July 25, 2012: http://seroproject.com/wp-content/uploads/2012/07/Sero-Preliminary-Data-Report_Final.pdf.

[7]   http://www.hpvinfo.ca/hpvinfo/professionals/overview-normal3.afpx.

[8] http://www.dentist-dentiste.com/canada5.htm.

"Worst of the Worst"? Queer Investments in Challenging Sex Offender Registries

[1] Despite its history as a generally white and classed referent and its implication in the erasure of transgender and transsexual identity, we use the term "queer" to encompass not just gay, lesbian, bisexual and transgendered identities but other non-heteronormative and non-gender nonconforming identifications as well.

[2] For information on Canadian carceral expansion, see Justin Piché work including his website updates at prisonstatecanada.blogspot.com and his 2010 report "Moratorium Needed on Punishment Legislation" available at the Canadian Center for Policy Alternatives website,

http://www.policyalternatives.ca/publications/monitor/moratorium-needed-punishment-legislation.

[3] A 2006 study by the Urban Institute charts the rarity of super-max prisons prior to 1986. However, by "2004, 44 states had supermax prisons" (Daniel P. Mears, March 2006). "Evaluating the Effectiveness of Supermax Prisons," Urban Institute p. ii, www.urban.org/UploadedPDF/411326_supermax_prisons.pdf). These institutions—which keep people incarcerated in solitary confinement cells from twenty-two to twenty-three hours a day—were made possible through public discourses about the "worst of the worst," criminals thought to constitute an imminent public danger.

[4] While the registry was a new initiative, increased surveillance of those categorized as sexual predators was not new. In 1997, Bill C-55 was implemented to allow the imposition of long-term supervision orders on offenders who are considered "likely" to re-offend but who do not meet the criteria for a "dangerous offender" designation. This had the effect of encompassing many convicted of lower level sex offenses within SO surveillance.

[5] Currently, the Canadian registry differs from its American counterpart in a few significant ways: a) the Canadian registry is accessible only to law enforcement officials and not to the general public, b) law enforcement officials may only access it for investigative purposes— (i.e. only after a crime has been committed), and c) the decision to add an individual onto the registry is not automatic but instead comes at the request of the Crown Counsel during sentencing.

[6] Canadian crime rates, including violent crime rates, have been decreasing steadily every year. In some provinces, the crime severity index in 2008 decreased by as much as 14 percent (Statistics Canada, 2011).

[7] William Eskridge. (2008). *Dishonorable Passions: Sodomy Laws in America.* New York: Viking, 82.

[8] *Ibid,* 81.

[9] This case, and Tommy Douglas and Pierre Trudeau's stance led to the 1969 decriminalization of homosexuality. (Kirkby, Gareth. 2006. "35 Years and Counting." *Extra West.* Retrieved online at: www.xtra.ca/public/National/35_years_and_counting-2303.aspx).

[10] HALO the Homophile Association of London Ontario with CLGRO the Coalition for Lesbian and Gay Rights in Ontario. "ON GUARD: A Critique of Project Gaurdian." September 1996 (HALO, 1996). Retrieved online at: www.clgro.org/pdf/On_Guard.pdf.

[11] Maria-Belén Ordóñez. (2010). "Taboo: Young Strippers and the Politics of Intergenerational Desire." P. 179 in *Sex, Drugs & Rock and Roll: Psychological, Legal and Cultural Examinations of Sex and Sexuality,* edited by Helen Gavin and Jacquelyn Bent. Oxford, UK: Inter-Disciplinary Press.

[12] Particularly for youth, state definitions of interpersonal and sexual violence are often complicit in the reproduction of heteronormativity. Through this alignment, anything external to gender conforming and heteronormative standards is framed as in need of regulation, punishment, and ultimately, containment. This contradiction is not new; state sponsored violence, marginalization, and criminalization has often been legitimated by claiming to offer 'protection' to women and (white) womanhood.

[13] Carlin DeGuerin Miller (March 24, 2010). "Sexting" Teens Are Being Labeled Sex Offenders, Lawmakers Look to Change That. CB News. Retrieved online at:

http://www.cbsnews.com/8301-504083_162-20001082-504083.html

[14] Canada recently became the first country to lay charges of first-degree murder (as well as the first to secure a conviction) for HIV non-disclosure.

[15] Ruth Wilson Gilmore. (2002). "Race and Globalization." In R. J. Johnson, Peter J. Taylor, Michael J. Watts, (Eds)., *Geographies of Global Change: Remapping the World*. Malden, MA., Blackwell Pub., 261.

[16] Eric Rofes "The Emerging Sex Panic Targeting Gay Men." Speech given at the National Gay and Lesbian Task Force's Creating Change Conference in San Diego, November 16, 1997.

[17] Roger Lancaster. (2011). *Sex Panic and the Punitive State*, University of California Press, 77.

[18] Rose Corrigan. (2006). "Making Meaning of Megan's Law." *Law & Social Inquiry* 31, 276.

[19] Wayne A. Logan. (2009). "Knowledge as Power: Criminal Registration and Community Notification Laws in America." Stanford University Press, 2009; FSU College of Law, Public Law Research Paper No. 387, 99.

[20] Cindy Struckman-Johnson and David Struckman-Johnson. (2000). "Sexual Coercion Rates in Seven Midwestern Prison Facilities for Men." *The Prison Journal*, December 2000 vol. 80 no. 4: 379-390

[21] See for example, recent work by Dany LaCombe including "Consumed with Sex: The Treatment of Sex Offenders in Risk Society," *The British Journal of Criminology*, Vol. 48, Issue 1, pp. 55-74 (2008).

[22] Lee Edelman. (2004). *No Future: Queer Theory and the Death Drive*. Durham, Duke University Press Books, 28.

[23] Roughly translated, PIAMP stands for Support Project for Minors Practicing Sex Work.

Contributors

Jack Aponte is a queer Boricua butch living in Brooklyn. Jack's preferred gender pronouns are she and her, but she doesn't mind other pronouns, either. Jack began over sharing and stirring shit up on the internet since the 90s; she blogged for many years at AngryBrownButch and, most recently, writes at jackalop.es. Jack is also a worker-owner at Palante Technology Cooperative, a NYC-based worker cooperative that helps community organizations and other nonprofits move forward with the aid of technology. She is involved in organizing and movements for social, economic, and media justice and in queer, trans, and people of color communities.

Sébastien Barraud, MA Anthropology, specialized in migration, ethnic and gay studies. He is an educator and union representative in a primary school. He is also a social worker at a drop in center for male sex workers. Born in France (1978), he has lived in Montreal since 2007. In 2005, he joined Warning, a think-tank originally from Paris and now also present in Brussels and Montreal, for which he has written more than 30 articles on-line and one about the impact of ethnicity for HIV prevention in *Santé gaie* (Peppers Ed.), the first French language book about gay men's health, published by Warning in 2010. Warning seeks to elaborate new ideas about the relations between gay men and their physical and mental health while taking account of the changes in LGBT lifestyles in western societies. From a position within the struggle against AIDS, Warning looks to renew issues linked to prevention and sexuality and the connections of those components with the notions of freedom, pleasure, desire, and norms. In 2009, Sébastien cofounded the Montreal activist collective PolitiQ-queers solidaires! and joined the organizing collective of Radical Queer Semaine, a ten day bilingual queer festival taking place every March in Montreal. Since 2011, he is also a member of the Canadian Feminist Alliance in Solidarity for sex workers rights.

Ryan Conrad is an outlaw artist, terrorist academic, and petty thief from a mill town in central Maine. He works through visual culture and performance to rupture the queer here and now in hopes of making time and space to imagine the most fantastic queer futures. His visual work is archived at www.faggotz.org and he is a co-founder of the Against Equality collective. He can be reached at rconrad@meca.edu.

James D'Entremont is a journalist and playwright based in Boston. His plays have been performed in Boston and New York, at regional theaters, and abroad. He is a Fellow of Yaddo, MacDowell, and the Albee Foundation. A longtime anti-censorship activist, he spent much of the 1990s heading the Boston Coalition for Freedom of Expression. More recently, he has joined his partner Bob Chatelle, executive director of the National Center for Reason and Justice, in working on behalf of Bernard Baran and others wrongfully convicted of crimes. He has written for publications ranging from *Index on Censorship* to *Passport* magazine. From 1996 to 2008, he was a staff writer for the gay men's monthly *The Guide*, contributing articles about censorship issues, sex-abuse controversies, day-care witch hunts, recovered-memory therapy, sex-offender legislation, and sex-offender treatment. His *Guide* assignments included coverage of the Paul Shanley sex-abuse trial.

Imani Keith Henry is a journalist for the progressive weekly, Workers' World newspaper. Since 1993, Imani has been a Staff Organizer at the International Action Center (IAC), where his activism has ranged from opposing U.S.-backed military inventions in Afghanistan, Colombia, Iran, Iraq, Haiti, Korea, Palestine, Somalia, Venezuela, and Yugoslavia to fighting to end the economic blockade of Cuba. Since 1995, Imani has been part of the national anti-police brutality and anti-death penalty movements in the United States and is one of the co-founders of Rainbow Flags for Mumia, a coalition of LGBTST people who demand the freedom of African-American political prisoner and journalist Mumia Abu Jamal. From 2002-2007 Imani toured with his multi-media theatre performance, B4T (before testosterone), across the North America and Europe. His writing has appeared in several publications including the Lambda Award winning *Does Your Mama Know* (Red Bone Press) and *Voices Rising: Celebrating 20 years of Black LGBT Writing* (Other Countries 2007) and *Marxism, Reparations and the Black Freedom Struggle*, (World View Forum Publishing). When Imani is not marching in the streets with the Occupy Movement or doing social media activism, he is finishing up a dual Masters degree at New York University. Imani Henry is a Caribbean transsexual male living in the Republic of Brooklyn, NY.

Jason Lydon is a Unitarian Universalist community minister in Boston, Massachusetts. He founded Black and

Pink after a short 6-month prison sentence and has been working in the movement to abolish the prison industrial complex for over a decade. When not organizing with others to overthrow imperialism, white supremacy, capitalism, and heteropatriarchy you can find Jason watching far too many movies or riding bikes. You can email him - Jason@blackandpink.org

Erica R. Meiners teaches, writes and organizes in Chicago. A participant in local and national justice work, specifically anti-militarization campaigns, prison abolition movements, and queer and immigrant rights organizing, she is the co-author of *Flaunt It! Queers organizing for public education and justice* (2009), and the author of *Right to be hostile: schools, prisons and the making of public enemies* (2009) and articles in *AREA Chicago, Meridians, Academe, Women's Studies Quarterly*, and *No More Potlucks*. A beekeeper and a long distance runner, she is also a member of American Federation of Teachers, University Professional of Illinois, Local 4100.

Liam Michaud works as a streetworker at CACTUS-Montréal, doing HIV and Hepatitis C prevention and advocacy among drug users, sex workers and those facing criminalization and state violence in Montréal. Over the last eight odd years he's been involved in projects working alongside those surviving the effects of incarceration, including the Prisoner Correspondence Project, and *Continuité-famille auprès des détenues*. He's doing research on displacement of communities living and working downtown through development and policing, and on failed public health responses to HIV in Québec.

Yasmin Nair is a Chicago-based writer, activist, academic, and commentator and a co-founder of Against Equality. The bastard child of queer theory and deconstruction, Nair's work has appeared in publications like *GLQ, The Progressive, make/shift, Time Out Chicago,* The Bilerico Project, *Windy City Times, Bitch, Maximum Rock'n'Roll,* and *No More Potlucks.* Her work also appears in various anthologies and journals, including *Captive Genders: Trans Embodiment and the Prison Industrial Complex, Singlism: What It Is, Why It Matters and How to Stop It, Windy City Queer: Dispatches from the Third Coast and Arab Studies Quarterly.* She is a member of the Chicago grassroots organization Gender JUST (Justice United for Societal Transformation). Nair is currently working on a book tentatively titled *Strange Love,* about neoliberalism and affect. Her website is www.yasminnair.net.

Josh Pavan is an Alberta-bred Canadian queen relocated to Montreal where she works as a trade unionist and community organizer. In 2007, he helped start up the Prisoner Correspondence Project, offering queer and trans specific support and resources to prisoners. His spare time is spent figuring out political drag as the divine Lady Gaza and defending the honor of misunderstood pop stars.

Liliana Segura is an journalist and editor writing on prisons and harsh sentencing. She is currently an associate editor at *The Nation Magazine.* lilianasegura.tumblr.com

Bridget Simpson, a Montreal-based invert, has done work with the Prisoner Correspondence Project since 2008.

Dean Spade is an associate professor at the Seattle University School of Law, currently a fellow in the Engaging Tradition Project at Columbia Law School. In 2002 he founded the Sylvia Rivera Law Project, a non-profit collective that provides free legal help to low-income people and people of color who are trans, intersex and/or gender non-conforming and works to build trans resistance rooted in racial and economic justice. He is the author of *Normal Life: Administrative Violence, Critical Trans Politics and the Limits of Law* (South End Press, 2011).

Unicorn Spell for Popularity

What you'll need:

10 Unicorn themed greeting cards
A range of coloured pens
The official Unicorn stamp
(or some Unicorn stickers should do)
10 sealable rainbow pouches (or envelopes)

What to do:

The Unicorn laws state that true popularity can only come from within. Begin by laying out your equipment; all the while considering 10 individuals you would like to reach out to. Taking your first Unicorn themed greeting card, write out an invitation, a poem, a story about your life – something that will deliver a piece of yourself to this person to really let them get to know you. Let your inner self get carried away with the spell, creating meaningful content using the colours that feel right for that person. Once you have finished, place your card inside a rainbow pouch (envelope), and finalise your spell with an official Unicorn stamp (or a Unicorn sticker). Now repeat this process for as many as 9 other special people, each time putting a piece of yourself into your greeting card, and sealing the spell in with your stamp/sticker. Deliver your cards to complete the spell.

Fun Fact:

Did you know that Unicorns make friends easier than any other creature on the planet? The Unicorn is the most approachable and friendly beast in the world making their popularity spell incredibly powerful.